on or before

w. _____

D0256901

THE
COMPLETE
PERSIAN

An early black Persian painted by Madame Henriette Ronner, a well-known French painter. Though sentimental in feeling, her work shows a keen knowledge of feline anatomy.

THE COMPLETE PERSIAN

by
Will Thompson and Eric Wickham-Ruffle

RINGPRESS

RINGPRESS

This edition first published in the United Kingdom in 1995 by
Ringpress Books Ltd,
PO Box 8, Lydney, Gloucestershire GL15 6YD.

© 1995 Cynthia Parzych Publishing, Inc.

Created and produced by Cynthia Parzych Publishing, Inc.
648 Broadway, New York, NY 10012
Editor: Cynthia Parzych
Cover design: Susan Hood
Text design: RCS Graphics

Discounts available for bulk orders
Contact the Special Sales Manager at
the above address.
Telephone 01594 563800.

ISBN 0 948955 79 1

CONTENTS

1. THE ANCESTRY OF THE PERSIAN CAT   11

2. EVOLUTION IN TERMS OF STYLE   31

3. HOW TO CHOOSE AND CARE FOR YOUR PERSIAN   51

4. PREPARING FOR YOUR NEW PERSIAN   69

5. REPRODUCTION   87

6. SHOWING AND JUDGING   113

7. THE PERSIAN STANDARD   137

8. A GALLERY OF BEAUTIFUL PERSIANS   177

9. THE PERSIAN AROUND THE WORLD   204

   CAT REGISTERIES AND ASSOCIATIONS   211

   GLOSSARY   213

   BIBLIOGRAPHY   218

   INDEX   220

For my parents who first taught me the meaning of love, giving, and sacrifice, and to all who have supported my ventures in the cat Fancy

W.T.

To John, whose support and encouragement during many long years made this book possible.

E.W.R.

ACKNOWLEDGEMENTS

I want to give special thanks to Allene Sergi and the staff of CFA Central Office for the help they gave at a moment's notice whenever I wanted to check some fact or needed a picture. The other American Cat Associations whose materials are referenced throughout this work also deserve thanks: ACA, ACFA, CFF and TICA. It is important, as well, to acknowledge and thank both Eric Wickham-Ruffle, my British associate from whom I have learned a great deal, and Cindy Parzych, my guide throughout the writing of this book for her patience, judgement, and good counsel. I must also thank all of the cat Fanciers of North and South America, Canada, Europe, Asia, Australasia, and, indeed, all the world, who have shown me that people do care–not only about the world but also about each other. And, of course, to all of my cat companions who agreed to share their far too short lives with me thereby making mine far richer and meaningful; they are with me even now.

Will Thompson, 1993

My warm thanks to Nicholas Snookes MRCVS for checking the veterinary details. I would like to acknowledge the help with background information which has been freely given by Jean Crockart, Joyce and Bob Worth, and Sheila Hamilton. I have been fortunate to enjoy the friendship and tuition of such towering figures of the past as Joan Thompson, Lily McVady, Marguerite Brunton, Dorrie Brice-Webb, and many others. I am indebted to them for the wealth of advice and information which they passed on to me over the years.

Eric Wickham-Ruffle, 1993

ABOUT THE AUTHORS

Will Thompson is one of America's leading authorities on the Persian cat as a result of many years experience as a breeder, exibitor, and judge of this breed. He is an all-breed judge of 30 years' standing for the Cat Fanciers' Association, a former Regional Director for the CFA, and most recently the CFA Treasurer. Will Thompson has also judged Persians internationally in Europe, Australia, New Zealand, and Japan. He has bred and exibited blue-point Himalayan, white, silver, and black-smoke Persians. His Himalayans were best in the United States for three successive years. A former Editor-in-Chief of *All Cats Magazine* and a contributor to two books, *The Cat Catalog* and *The Noble Cat,* he has appeared on television, radio programs, and in motion pictures about cats. He is also a lecturer on the subject.

Eric Wickham–Ruffle has a reputation as one of the great judges of pedigreed cats in Britain and Europe. His particular expertise is the Persian, where his knowledge and experience is regarded as second to none outside the United States. For many years, he was a leading breeder of Chinchilla Persians. He was formerly Chairman and is now Patron of the Longhaired (Persian) Cat Club in Britain. He is Vice President of the West of Scotland Cat Club and also Vice President of the Bucks Oxon and Berks Cat Clubs. Eric Wickham-Ruffle was a member of the Executive of the Governing Council of the Cat Fancy for many years, where he was secretary of the committee responsible for appointing all the longhair (Persian) judges in Britain and is one of the four trustees in whom the property of the GCCF is vested. He is currently President of the Kensington Kitten and Neuter Cat Club and President of the Red Cream and Tortie Cat Club, two of the oldest cat clubs in Britain. Eric Wickham-Ruffle has judged at cat shows in more than 20 countries and is one of only two Honorary Judges in Britain for FIFe, the international feline organization.

Louis Wain, the society painter of cats, recorded the winners, mostly Persians, at the 1890 Crystal Palace show. Wain became president of The National Cat Club in England when Harrison Weir, the founder of the cat Fancy, retired from that position.

CHAPTER I

THE ANCESTRY OF THE PERSIAN CAT

Of all the companion animals, perhaps the most controversial has always been the cat, *Felis domesticus*—and of all the breeds of *Felis*, the Persian has always been the subject of more comment, more contention, and at the same time more admiration than any other breed. It was the simple, common cat, Muezza, that was the beloved companion of Mohammed; Gavroche, the magnificent Angora, that welcomed Victor Hugo home on his return from exile; Hodge, the cat of unknown ancestry

Gavroche (also called Chanoine) was the beloved Angora pet of well-known French novelist Victor Hugo, author of Les Misèrables. The Angora is one of the three breeds from which today's Persian developed.

that was the friend of the great Dr. Samuel Johnson; and it was the simple house cat that symbolized all that Mark Twain believed to be essential for a happy home—each represents that which is loved in any cat. Yet, the cat is also anathema to those who would control others. The domesticated cat has come to surpass the well-loved dog as man's most popular animal companion, and of all the cat breeds, the Persian is the most popular. Hundreds of millions of dollars are spent every year caring for these welcome guests who share the lives of so many.

THE COMPANION FOR OUR CULTURE

The present day need for a hunting or herding companion has lessened. The companionship of the cat better suits the lifestyles of our culture where busy, stress-laden members prefer relaxing with the discerning cat companion rather than with the more subservient dog. The cat's ability to take care of itself when provided with the Spartan necessities of food, water, warmth, and a simple tray of sand is most attractive. Cats readily adjust to the lifestyles of their human companions. Contrasted with the complex day-to-day requirements of the canine, which include walking and general exercise, cleaning, sanitation, and amusement, it is the domestic cat, *Felis domesticus*, which best fulfills our need for animal companionship in these busy times.

EARLY EVIDENCE OF DOMESTICATION

The exact point in time when the cat became domesticated is unknown. Among early artifacts—the famous cave drawings of Altamira and Lascaux, the pictographic records of Australia's Ayer's Rock and the southwestern United States, the carvings found throughout Africa, Asia, and Oceania, the Mayan glyphs and codices—the cat as a companion to humans is not depicted. No bones, no teeth have been found in the rubbish heaps of ancient habitats revealing any record of companion cats. Pictured with amazing sophistication are the records of early culture's romance and fascination with the dog, the horse, the deer, and even the bear, but among all of these early records, no trace of the cat sharing the firesides in these primitive cultures is to be found. The domesticated cat is conspicuous only by its absence from the life of early man as we know it today. It is in Egypt where we find the first evidence of the cat's domestication in about 2000 B.C. Paintings and inscriptions dating from 2000 B.C. show cats in conditions which suggest primitive domestication in Egypt and there is plenty of evidence that the Egyptians kept cats domestically. Cats were revered and protected and after their deaths, interred in special cemeteries. They were deified in the cult of the goddess Bast, or Pasht. This is clearly the derivation of our word "puss". After existing for nearly 2000 years, the cult of Bast began to decline in about 350 B.C. The cult was finally banned by imperial decree in 35 A.D. But the custom of keeping cats spreadly slowly, nevertheless, throughout the Middle East. We find evidence of domestication in records from ancient India and

The goddess Bast, shown as a woman with a feline head, holding in her right hand a musical instrument, and a shield in the left. She symbolized the light, warmth, and energy of the sun. The other side of character was the night-loving and mysterious part of the cat's nature linked with moon worship.

This Roman carving in stone of a young girl from the first or second century A.D. is one of the earliest pieces of evidence for domestication of the cat in Europe.

13

China. It was the Romans who introduced domestic cats to Europe. European explorers and adventurers, in turn, carried them to other parts of the world. They were taken along on long journeys as companions and pest destroyers. These early beginnings have resulted in the strong influence of Europe in the world of cats.

The history of the cat family has been traced through fossil records to the Lower Oligocene Epoch about 40 million years ago. The mammalian pattern identified as that of the cat appears to have been established very early in the evolution of modern mammals. At a time when the distant ancestors of most mammals were hardly recognizable, the cat's pattern was already established. Those mammals which we would recognize as resembling a twentieth century cat, however, would not appear on the world's stage for about another thirty million years. These cats of about ten million years ago have evolved relatively unchanged.

PREHISTORIC ANCESTORS

The cat of today can probably trace its ancestry to an early mammal which lived about fifty million years ago. It was the size of a lynx and probably developed in Asia from where it spread to other parts of the Continent. There are, however, many cloudy and mysterious developmental paths along which the modern cat may have trodden during the several million years during which it evolved. Specific details of the domestic cat's development are conjecture and have been debated and discussed for many years.

In 1881, with the publication in London of his monumental book, *The Cat*, Dr. St. John Mivart, Ph.D., F.R.S., produced a work which for the first time considered all the possible aspects of the cat including lengthy analyses of the cat's physiognomy, physiology, psychology, history, and development as well as a complex, but inconclusive discussion, of the cat's phylogeny. While this volume is still considered to be a valuable reference for those interested in cats, many of Mivart's ideas about the origins of the cat have been proven incomplete or incorrect. The tremendous scientific growth during the past several decades has provided far more accurate conclusions than those reached by Dr. Mivart.

It is believed by most experts that cats evolved from mammals that became dominant following the disappearance of the great dinosaurs. Among these mammals were the great hunters, the *Carnivorae*. The cat as we know it today descends from this group that also included dog-like animals such as foxes, wolves, bear, weasels, skunks, and otters and cat-like animals such as genets, civets, mongooses, and hyenas. More important, the *Carnivorae* included the ancestral big cats, both great and small such as the lion, tiger, cheetah, lynx, ocelot, and margay. One of the distinctive features of these carnivorous mammals was their teeth used as tools for cutting and tearing meat.

These distinctive teeth were also present in the early fish-eating mammals, the *Creodonts*. *Creodonts* were prevalent about fifty million years ago, not so very long ago when it is considered that the earth is thought to be four billion years old. The *Creodonts* were one of the groups that did not survive until historic times. However, there is another offshoot from this early group that did. The members of this genetic off-shoot had teeth that were arranged for cutting and tearing, but which, importantly, were also more efficient than those of the *Creodonts*. Additionally, their bodies were more muscular and athletic, and their brains were larger. These were the *Miacids* who became prevalent about forty-five million years ago. Modern scientists believe the members of today's cat family descend from the *Miacids*.

WHAT'S IN A NAME

In the London Zoo in 1916, Mr. R. I. Pocock divided today's cats into two major groups based upon one simple attribute: whether a cat is able to purr. It is the development of the hyoid bone in any cat that deter-mines whether that cat can purr or not. The larger cats, which Mr. Pocock placed in the genus *Panthera,* include the lion, the tiger, the leopard, and the jaguar. These cats cannot purr because the hyoid structure simply is not developed. Instead, cats of this genus roar. Additionally, their eyes have round pupils.

Pocock's second group contains those cats in which the develop-ment of the hyoid bone enables purring; additionally, most of the members of this genus have vertical pupils. This second genus, *Felis,* includes numerous kinds of small cats including both the mountain lion and the domestic cat. All cats, except the cheetah, have retractile claws and for this reason, the cheetah is placed in a separate genus, *Acinonyx.* Some authorities also place the Canadian lynx and bobcat in an added, separate genus, *Lynx.*

It is also interesting to note that Douglas Richardson, of the London Zoo staff, confirms this basic difference: the cats which can roar (*Panthera*) cannot purr; the cats which can purr (*Felis*) cannot roar. The difference lies in a group of bones which link the larynx to the skull. In the big cats they have cartilage in the two chains of bones, which is very elastic and this gives sufficient flexibility in the vocal apparatus to length-en the air column. This, in conjunction with a pad of elastic tissue at the end of the vocal folds enables the animal to roar.

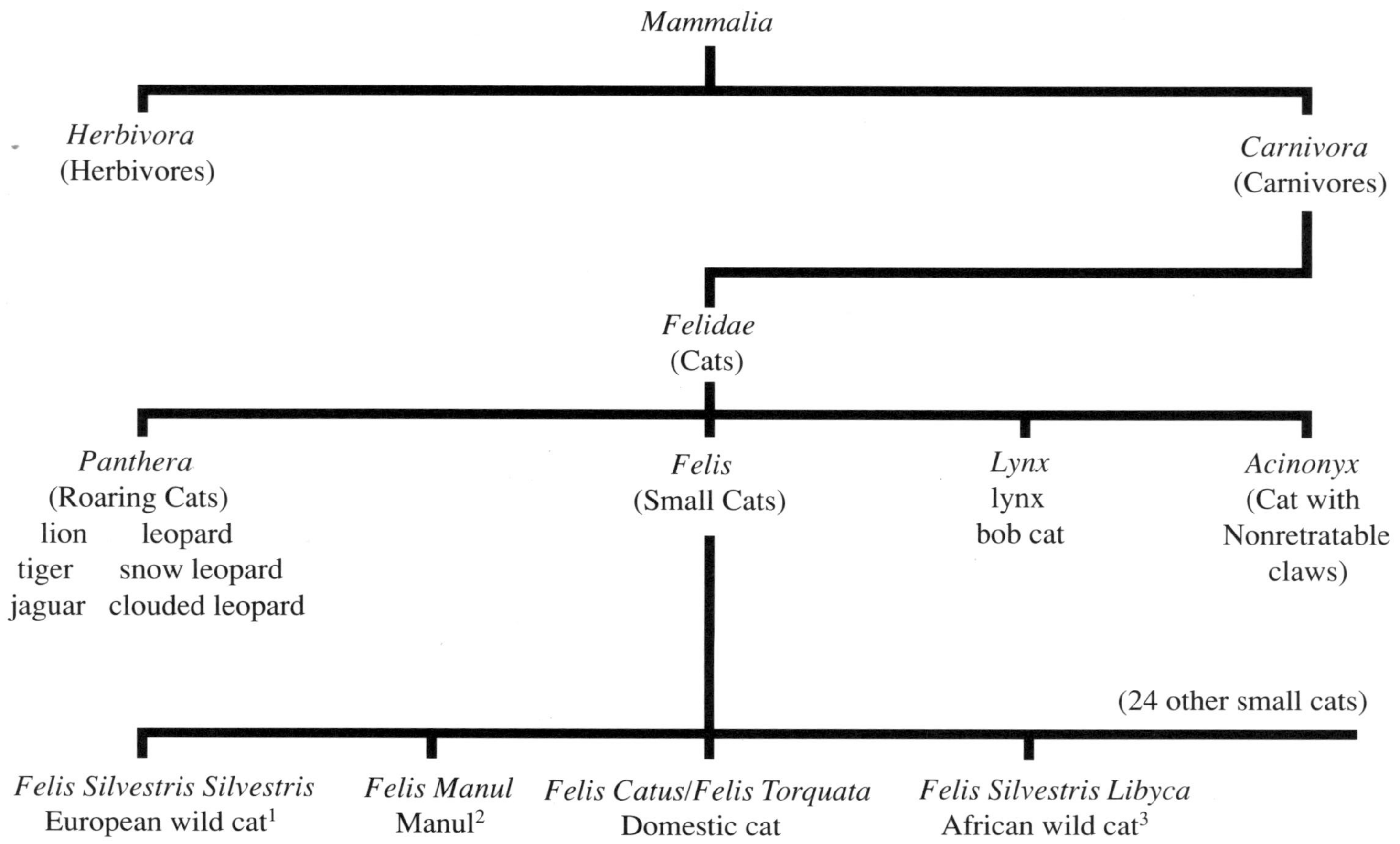

Mammalia

Herbivora
(Herbivores)

Carnivora
(Carnivores)

Felidae
(Cats)

Panthera
(Roaring Cats)
tiger   snow leopard
lion   leopard
jaguar   clouded leopard

Felis
(Small Cats)

Lynx
lynx
bob cat

Acinonyx
(Cat with
Nonretratable
claws)

Felis Silvestris Silvestris
European wild cat[1]

Felis Manul
Manul[2]

Felis Catus/Felis Torquata
Domestic cat

Felis Silvestris Libyca
African wild cat[3]

(24 other small cats)

[1] This cat may have bred with early domesticated cats that reached Europe
[2] A possible ancestor of longhair cats including the Persian
[3] This cat is the most likely ancestor of the domestic cat

16

In the smaller cats (*Felis*) the chain of bones is ossified so that they cannot give full-throated roars. Any attempt to do so produces a sort of screaming sound. They can, however, purr continuously on both incoming and outgoing breaths. The purring is produced by the vibration of membranes close to the vocal chords.

Sir David Attenborough, the well-known zoologist, disagrees. "Lions and tigers certainly purr — I've heard them myself. I was unsure as to how widespread purring was, and so checked and discovered to my surprise that the ability is ever more widespread than I had thought. Apparently black bears and hyenas do as well!" Attenborough's research reveals that the young of many species purr as they suckle.

The most current, scientific nomenclature classifies cats into two main groups: small cats, *Felini*, and large cats, *Pantherini*. The small cats include fifteen genera with twenty-eight species; the big cats include two genera: *Uncia* (the snow leopard) and *Panthera* which includes four species (leopard, jaguar, tiger, and lion). It is the *Felini* in which we are interested; this is the group that includes the Persian and all domestic cats.

The domestic cat, including the Persian, is commonly referred to as *Felis domesticus*, but this classification is incorrect. The founder of modern scientific nomenclature, Swedish botanist Professor Carl von Linné, who published his seminal work in the 1750s, classified the domestic cat *Felis catus*. This, of course, would be totally acceptable except for the fact that Professor von Linné used this designation to identify the blotched or classic tabby-patterned cat while ignoring the equally identifiable and widespread mackerel-tabby-patterned cats. Experts use the classification *Felis torquata* to pin the matter down completely. The resulting *F. domesticus*, *F. catus* (blotched or classic tabby pattern), and *F. torquata* (the mackerel-tabby-patterned cat) present quite a mouthful – but are precise. *Felis domesticus* will most certainly suffice as an identifier for the cat as we know it including the prized Persian.

THE SOURCE OF THE PERSIAN BREED

Scholars believe that Egypt is the most probable place for the cat's domestication about 2000 B.C. This first, domesticated cat is thought to be a distant relative of *Felis silvestris libyca,* which is generally known as the African Wild Cat. This is a small, buff-colored cat with darker stripes which today is found throughout Africa and in Asia, from the Middle East to India. It is about ten to eighteen pounds in weight and often lives close to human settlements. The African Wild Cat's kittens can be tamed.

The actual lineage of the Persian cat will probably never be known, but most experts agree that longhaired cats, including the Persian,

Queen Tiyi, wife of Amenhopet III (c. 1411–1375 B.C.), the great Egyptian pharoah, seated in her papyrus canoe with her favorite cat beneath her chair. The Egyptians were the first known civilization to welcome cats into their homes.

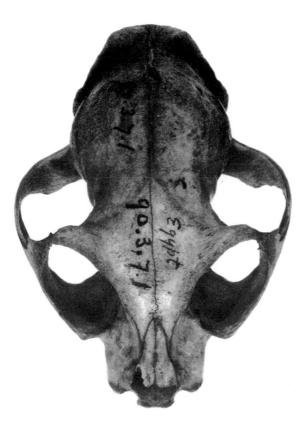

This is the one remaining skull from a consignment of 300,000 cat mummies excavated at the site of Beni Hassan in Egypt in the nineteenth century. Most of these were exported to Liverpool, England and sadly disposed of as fertilizer for farmland.

are the result of a genetic mutation. The longhair variety of cat was probably the result of mating between the European Wild Cat and Pallas's Cat also known as the Steppe Cat. The European Wild Cat weighs about ten to twenty-four pounds and lives in parts of Europe and Western Asia. It keeps well away from people and the kittens are not tamable. Pallas's Cat *(Felis manul)* was named after the German naturalist, Peter Simon Pallas, who discovered the cat around the Caspian Sea area. Pallas claimed these cats like to mate with domestic cats and thought they might be ancestors of the longhaired breeds because their coats are longer and more dense that the coats of other wild *Felis* species, giving the coat more insulation from the snow and frozen ground which is its habitat. They are also known as the Steppe Cat because they come from the steppes of Central Asia. These are usually quite wild and vicious cats.

The European Wild Cat which still can be found in remote parts of Europe to western Eurasia, bears a slight resemblance in its coat's thickness and length to the modern Persian.

Pallas's cat is one of the more likely candidates in the ancestry of the modern Persian.

That mutations do occur in cats with surprising frequency is seen in the many genetic mutations that have occurred since the founding of the Cat Fanciers' Association in America in 1906. Recent mutations that have been recognized for championship status and pedigreed registry in the United States and Europe are the Cornish Rex, the Devon Rex, the Scottish Fold, the American Wirehair, and the American Curl.

The last three are not currently recognized by the GCCF (Governing Council of the Cat Fancy) in Britain or by the Feline International Federation, FIFe. Each of these, while being classed as a shorthaired breed (except for the American Curl that occurs in the long-haired as well as the shorthaired variation), is recognized as a separate, viable breed. There have also appeared cats which many believe to be longhair mutations including the Balinese (a longhair variation of the Siamese), and the Somali (the longhair variant of the Abyssinian).

Other longhair varieties have been developed by knowledgeable breeders through the careful application of sound genetic principles. Included in this category are the Javanese, the longhair version of the col-orpoint shorthair breed; the Cymric, the longhair variant of the Manx; and longhair variants of the Scottish Fold and Japanese Bobtail breeds respec-tively. None of these is recognized in Great Britain or in the European cat Fancy. There is little doubt that an early mutation was a change in the hair length of the cat.

It is important to point out that the cat Fancy in America separates all domestic cats into two major groups: longhair cats, and shorthair cats. The cat Fancy in other parts of the world further subdivides these groups into longhair, semi-longhair, shorthair and Siamese, and/or Oriental cats.

The major longhair varieties recognized by the American cat Fancy are the American Curl, the Balinese, the Birman, the Javanese, the Maine Coon Cat, the Norwegian Forest Cat, the Persian, the Somali, and the Turkish Angora. Currently under consideration as longhair breeds are the Rag Doll, the Turkish Van, the Oriental Longhair, and the Siberian. While some of these cats have coats which most agree would classify as semi-longhaired, the placement of each on the show bench and into the pedigree registry is different among cat registering bodies in America, Europe and Great Britain.

Breeders are continuing their efforts to enrich the world of domes-tic cats through experimental breed crosses aimed at producing newer and more exotic varieties of longhaired cats. There are breeders working to produce a longhaired variety of Burmese that some have christened the Tiffany. This has already received preliminary recognition by the GCCF in Britain, and many beautiful examples are now appearing on the British show bench.

A longhair variant of the Rex has also appeared from time to time. The first example appeared in the late 1960s and was exhibited by the famous Rodell Rex Cattery of Bob and Dell Smith in southern California. The cat was a red-mackerel tabby and white longhaired Rex which the Smiths christened as the Marcel breed. This cat was the progeny of a female Rex mutant discovered in southern California named Mystery Lady. Unfortunately, because of lack of interest on the part of breeders, the cat was neutered without any further work to develop this exciting variation.

There is also a newer variant that has tentatively been called the Dalles Rex as it was bred in the vicinity of Dalles, Oregon. Some breeders call this mutation the Alpaca cat because its fur has the texture of the coat of the Alpaca, the llama originally found in South America. The cat's fur is about one inch in length and hangs in loose ringlets. The Dalles Rex or Alpaca is medium to quite long in body, and stands very high on leg. This variety also has oversized paws.

Work is currently in progress in the United States that has produced a longhaired variety of the Japanese Bobtail. The main rule in creating new varieties of cats seems to be that a breeder will develop a new variant if it fills a gap in any physical attribute (such as coat, color, conformation, etc.) in the spectrum of domesticated cats that is already recognized as desirable and beautiful.

PROBABLE ANCESTRY

There probably was a mutation in the coat length of the cat that was to become the ancestor of today's Persian. For centuries, the Europeans referred to all longhair cats as Persians or Angoras. The two names were essentially interchangeable. Dr. St. John Mivart, the English naturalist in his important work of 1881, *The Cat*, states, "The Angora, or Persian cat, is remarkable for its great size, and for the length and delicacy of its hair, especially the belly and throat. Most commonly its coat is of uniform white yellowish or greyish color, while the soles of its paws and its lips are often flesh-colored. Its temperament is said to be sometimes exceptionally lethargic; but this is certainly not always the case, and may be due to excessive petting for generations. This breed is believed by some naturalists to be descended from an Asiatic wild cat, with a shorter tail than that of the Egyptian cat." Dr. Mivart footnotes another important feline authority, Pallas, who states in his work, *Zoographia Russo-Siberia*, "...cats like the Angora are brought to Siberia from China." The important point is that Dr. Mivart identifies the longhair Angora and Persian as being the same cat.

EARLY AMERICAN REGISTRATIONS

In the June 15, 1903 edition of *The Cat Journal*, A. St. John Oliver wrote an article, "A Word For the Golden State". In the article the author states: "Many of the California Persian Angoras (for the breeds have become inextricably intermixed in spite of some special standards by which it is claimed they can be distinguished), are allowed great freedom, and some even roam at night, and very regular in their habits do they become. One fine white male has a certain tree in the world famous Golden Gate Park, where he may generally be found at a certain hour each day, sitting among the branches as large as a spitz dog, for which he has often been mistaken."

It should be of no surprise, then, that the Cat Fanciers' Association, Inc., the world's largest pedigreed cat registry, indicated on their registration (pedigree) forms, "Longhair-Persian or Angora" for breed identification purposes until the 1950s. The terms Angora and Persian were synonymous. They indicated the same breed of cat since the two had been interbred until they could no longer be differentiated as separate breeds. This also identified the practice of cat breeders of interbreeding longhair cats for many years before the beginning of the cat Fancy in America. On May 8, 1895, Englishman J. T. Hyde organized the first American cat show. It was held at Madison Square Garden in New York City. America's first cat club, the American Cat Club, was formed by a group of cat lovers following this first show. Ultimately, from these early beginnings the Persian breed predominated and became today's most popular and prized pedigreed cat.

It was made clear in the 1940s that there were other types of longhaired cats when the authorities of the Ankara Zoo in Turkey established a valuable colony for the Turkish Angora cat. The cats of this breed differ greatly from the Persian in both coat and conformation. It was from this colony that Colonel Walter Grant and his wife, Lisa, obtained permission from the Turkish Government to bring breeding pairs of these prized Turkish Angora cats with them to the United States. The Grants worked with these cats and exhibited them in the 1960s at club meetings in California to obtain support for their recognition by CFA for registration and show in America. These cats were the ancestors of the cats currently registered and shown in the United States as Turkish Angoras.

Additionally, the first Turkish Van cats were brought into Great Britain in 1955 by Laura Lushington. They were named Turkish Vans since they originally came from the Lake Van district of Turkey. They are semi-longhairs, and quite different from Angoras. They caused quite a lot of comment in the daily papers as the public was fascinated by their delight in water. It was claimed that the Turkish Vans enjoyed a daily swim.

The breed names, Persian and Angora, certainly support the widely-held belief that the longhaired cats which we call Persians today originated in Asia. Unlike the modern practice of giving some breeds an exotic-sounding name to increase the breed's appeal (such as calling the longhaired Siamese variant a Balinese because the cat's movements reminded one early Balinese breeder of the beautiful, sinuous movements of Balinese temple dancers), during the seventeenth and eighteenth centuries cat lovers were inclined to assign breed names based on the perceived place of origin of the breed itself. Early breeders believed that the Persian originated in Persia, and the Angora in Ankara, Turkey.

FROM THE RECENT PAST

The French publication, *Histoire Naturelle Générale et Particulière,* Paris, 1749-1803, by the Comte de Buffon, is often cited as an authoritative source of information about felines. In an excerpt from this work, "Les Voyages de Pietro della Valle," Mr. della Valle (who lived from 1586 until 1652) alludes not only to the Angora cat, but also to a longhaired breed of cat originating in the Persian province of Chorazan (now identified as Khorasan, a section bordering modern Afghanistan). This early Italian world traveler describes Persian cats as being gray (the color modern cat Fanciers refer to as blue) with coats that were fine, glossy, long, and silky. The hair was curly in places and especially on the chest. He describes the tail as having hair five to six inches in length. These cats, according to della Valle, were taken by the Portuguese into India. He planned to take four breeding pairs back home to Italy when he returned.

The naturalist Nicholas-Claude Fabri de Peiresc brought long-haired cats from Angora (today known as Ankara, Turkey) to France in the sixteenth century. These were described "... as colored, dun and speckled cats, beautiful to behold." They had long, silky coats and were of slim build. They were bred and some of the kittens were taken to England where they were to become known as French Cats. Some years later heavier-boned cats with long coats arrived in Europe from Persia (today known as Iran). The two types of cats were interbred quite indiscriminately.

Most experts agree that the longhaired cat was well established in Europe by the sixteenth or, at the latest, the early seventeenth century with the Angora probably arriving first and the Persian following soon after. In 1856, a letter sent home to France by Lottin de la Val describes the Angora cat of Armenia. Monsieur de la Val portrays the Angora as being white, gray, or orange-spotted in color and found in Kurdistan and Baghdad. These are the cats which are among the ancestors of today's Persian breed. Other early authorities refer to another longhaired variety of cat, the Russian Longhair. Dr. Mivart identifies another variety which he calls the blue or Carthusian cat: "The blue or Carthusian cat is a breed with long, soft hair of a uniform, dark greyish-blue tone, with black lips, and black soles to the paws." These, too, are possibly ancestors of today's Persians.

The Persian was described in the last century and earlier as being a heavier cat with a larger, rounder head, a shorter nose, and a thicker, less silky coat than the Angora. The Angora was portrayed as a more refined, lighter-boned, longer-nosed, larger-eared cat whose coat was made up of long, silky fur. The Russian Longhair had a very dense, long coat, large and prominent eyes, a very large body with relatively short legs, and a tail with hair that was the same length from the base to the tip.

This Angora, illustrated by Harrison Weir in the late 1800s, shows the long, fine quality of fur which we associate with the early forerunners of the Persian breed.

THE ANGORA CAT

In 1900, H. Winslow described the Angora cat in her book, *Concerning Cats*. She stated that this cat originated in Angora in western Asia, the same area that is famed for its goats which produce long hair of the same fine quality. Known today as Ankara, Turkey, Angora was home to this early breed of longhaired cat. The Standard ·of the early 1900's required the Angora to have a small head with not too long a nose; large eyes that should harmonize in color with the coat color (the cats came in many colors), small, pointed ears with a tuft of hair at the apex; and a very full mane around the neck. It was this mane that was referred to in early literature as the Lord Mayor's Chain or, as Robert Kent James called it in his book published in 1898, *The Angora Cat,* the Queen Elizabeth Ruffle. James refers to only three colors of Angora: white, black, and buff; other writers specifically mention the color blue. The legs of the Angora cat were described as being moderate in length but giving the appearance of being shorter than they truly were because of the cat's long coat. Harrison Weir, the father of the cat Fancy, chose as his favorite color of Angora, the blue-eyed white. He also listed orange-eyed blacks, slates and blues, light fawns (creams), deep reds, mottled grays, and smokes as being colors of the Angora.

THE RUSSIAN LONGHAIR CAT

It is in his book *Our Cats and All About Them* that Harrison Weir wrote about the Russian Longhair cat he once owned. He described this

This cat with Russian Longhair characteristics was owned by Mrs Finch of Maldon, Essex, England. It was illustrated in *Daniel's Rural Sports* in 1813. Its massive size, powerful physique, and a tail resembling that of a fox made it a very unusual specimen. In fact Mrs. Finch was offered one hundred pounds for the cat the equivalent of one hundred fifty dollars, an immense sum for that time.

breed as larger in body and with shorter legs than either the Persian or the Angora. The cat's mane was very large, long, and dense, somewhat woolly in texture but with coarse hairs in it. The cat's color was that of a dark tabby; however, the markings were not a decided black color nor were they dark and sound. The ground color lacked the richness of color found in the Persian. The Russian Longhair's eyes were described as large, prominent, and bright orange, but slightly tinted with green. The ears were described as large with small tufts, and full of long, woolly hair (furnishings). The tail, from the base to the tip, was very short and covered with thick even-length hair resembling that of the British wild cat. All Russian Longhair cats as described by Harrison Weir were brown tabbies with an occasional black appearing.

In *Concerning Cats*, H. Winslow briefly mentioned the Russian Longhair. She stated that the cat was fond of cold weather and the breed's fur was more dense than the Angora thereby indicating that it was used to colder regions. Perhaps it is this Russian Longhair that is a relative of the Steppe Cat. She goes on to state that, "Many of the cats we see are crosses of Angora and Persian, or Angora and Russian, so that it is extremely difficult to know a thoroughbred cat which has not been mixed with other varieties."

THE PERSIAN CAT

In *Concerning Cats*, Winslow also describes the Persian cat as all black. "It has a very fluffy frill, or Lord Mayor's Chain, and orange eyes. Next to him comes a light slate or blue Persian with yellow eyes. The fur of the Persian is much more woolly than that of the Angora and sometimes in hot weather mats easily." She also mentions that the Persian's tail is much fuller and not easily compressed into a small space; it has a larger head than the Angora, and its ears are less pointed. The ear of the Persian, she felt should have a small tuft at the end and be well-furnished with long hair inside. "It is usually larger in body and apparently stronger made, although slender and elegant in appearance with small bones and graceful in movement."

AN ALCHEMIST'S AMALGAM

It is from these three separate breeds, the Angora, the Russian Longhair, and the Persian of the past that today's Persian Cat has developed. The early Persians had longer noses, and larger ears, which did not fit into the rounded contour of the head. The general effect was of a

In 1889 Harrison Weir, in his "Standards of Excellence and Beauty," illustrated a blue long-hair which begins to resemble the modern Persian, apart from its large ears and a slightly wedge–shaped head.

wedge-shaped head, lacking the full, broad muzzle of today's best Persians. It is from cats with less luxurious coats, different body and structural styles that the compact, flowing-coated Persian of today was refined and developed. The three foundation breeds each provided part of the mixture which has resulted in the beautiful Persian cat of today. It is highly likely that the areas surrounding Ankara in Turkey, Khorasan in Iran, Afghanistan, and Baghdad and Kurdistan in Iraq, were the birth places of the Persian cat's ancestors. In these areas of the world, where weather conditions can be quite cold, the longhair variant would have been most comfortable. Some modern scholars point out that the Persian, with its smaller ears and rounded head, is best able to deal with colder climates; the shorthair varieties often have very large ears and longer heads providing more surface area from which these varieties are better able to dispel body heat in very warm or hot climates. Scholars argue that the longhaired Persian must be related to Pallas's Cat whose general head and ear shape resembles that of the Persian. Pallas's Cat is small and longhaired; has small, rounded ears; short legs, and a compact body suggesting that it should be considered a likely ancestor of the Persian cat.

THE MOST PROBABLE ANSWER

At some unknown point in time then, either a mutation or a natural cross between smaller, wild cat breeds occurred which produced long fur in cats. These cats, which ultimately became domesticated, probably originated in the Middle East, in the areas surrounding modern-day Turkey, Iran, and Afghanistan. These progenitors of the Persian were brought to Europe about 300 years ago through Italy and France by early travelers. These early longhairs were interbred, and ultimately, natural selection encouraged those qualities which were hardy and vigorous. Early cat breeders doubtless chose those qualities which they considered to be of great beauty such as color, coat length, and the general appearance of their cats.

With the advent of a formal cat Fancy in the mid-to-late 1800s and its written rules and descriptions of what the Persian cat should be in color, coat, and conformation, early breeders began the genetic selection which created the magnificent Persian. Breeders, applying their knowledge of the laws of genetics produced over the past 100 years the beautiful Persian of today. Cat lovers and those who appreciate beauty for the sheer love of beauty cherish these gorgeous Persian cats whose very name conjures a thing of beauty or something mysterious and artistic.

The Persian Standard was created in England to describe the perfect blue Persian by Harrison Weir. This blue, bred by Mrs. Wells of Isleworth, England, could have been the model for that first Standard. Mrs. Wells was one of the first exhibitors of blues which were noted for "their wonderfully fine coats."

CHAPTER II

EVOLUTION IN TERMS OF STYLE

Harrison Weir is considered the
father of the cat Fancy.

There was obviously a beginning for the creation of the Persian
Standard. Originally it was created in England to describe the perfect blue
Persian.

Harrison Weir, a well-known artist, cat lover, and fellow of the
Royal Horticultural Society, built up a store of information on cats over a
long period of time. He studied cats for about half a century and in 1889
published a book entitled *Our Cats*, in which he gave the first Standards
for all recognized breeds and colors. He called these "Points of
Excellence." In the English cat Fancy of the mid-to-late 1800s, the male
blue Persian was considered to be the best of all Persians in appearance,
coat color, coat length, bone structure, and overall look. The blue was a
favorite of Queen Victoria who owned two. Besides the blue, the other
Persian colors recognized in 1901 by the British cat Fancy were black,

white, orange, cream, smoke, spotted tabby, Chinchilla, tortoiseshell, bi-color, and tri-color. When the Governing Council of the Cat Fancy (GCCF) was founded in England in 1910, it was determined that Persians should be called longhairs, a decision that has stood in Great Britain to the present.

Puck III, an early Chinchilla was owned by the Princess Victoria of Schleswig-Holstein, the patron of The National Cat Club in London. She kept this male at Cumberland Lodge in Windsor.

THE PERSIAN OF 1909

Persians were introduced from England into North America during the last two decades of the nineteenth century. By the early 1900s the Persian had overtaken the Maine Coon Cat as the principal longhair at shows in the United States. American breeders initially followed the Standards established by their British counterparts. In the 1909 book, *Everybody's Cat Book*, D. B. Champion describes the perfect show-type Persian as follows: " The head should be round, the face short, the nose should be snubby and have a good stop — that is to say, the nose should have a decided break in the middle to make it *retroussé* in appearance, the cheeks, and under the eyes, should be round and full; the eyes large and round and set straight in the head; they should not be angular in any way; the ears should be small and set well-apart, pointing somewhat forward

32

and well-tufted; the body should be cobby and very deep and broad in the chest, and the back as straight as possible; the legs should be set low down, and not continue up to the top of the shoulders...the hair should be as long as possible,...the legs should be short and thick...the tail should be short enough to be carried slightly away from the body, but not touching the ground or turning upwards at the end...."

It is amazing to read this 1909 description of the Persian cat in relation to today's Standards for the breed. A review shows that the Persian Standard has not changed very much in nearly one hundred years of breeding Persian cats for show. There is one major point of difference in the basic approach to the cat Fancy's Persian Standard of 1909 and today's Standards in America. In 1909, each Persian color was assigned a separate scale of points thereby treating each color as if it were a separate breed. Today's Standard in America judges all colors and patterns of Persian using the same scale of points.

SOLID COLORS

In the *Cat Journal*, published in the United States in 1903, H. F. Vidal noted, " The white class in our shows is generally one of the best filled, that is, in quality, notwithstanding the fact that on the continent the

Crystal, a blue-eyed white female, owned by Miss M. Hunt, was considered in 1903, "the best blue-eyed white female" in the United Kingdom. Miss Hunt purchased Crystal in 1898, when she was four months old and considered the cat a good investment since Crystal was only once beaten by another white cat in the show ring.

preference is generally for warmer colors." Vidal goes on to say that in the Arab stables of the Rajahs of India there were many white cats, more prized if they had odd eyes, one pink and the other blue. It was the belief, at the time, that white Persians were "in a partial state of albinism," partial since the blue and sometimes golden eyes of these white Persian's demonstrated that the normal pink eyes of the albino had been eliminated through selective breeding. Vidal also reported that "some of our best cats are imported from Persia."

In 1909, expert opinion was that "... the eyes in this variety make or mar the cat; they should be either deep blue or dark orange, any pale yellow or green tinge being incorrect and very objectionable." And again, reference was made to the superiority of imported white Persians. The cats imported from India were thought to be of the best quality and were very superior to the ordinary Persian. These cats were described as having a long, trailing coat; snub face; short, thick legs; beautifully tufted ears and toes; and cobby in shape. However, they were not considered strong in physique perhaps from being too inbred which "... reduces the size but improves the quality."

While the black Persian had proven to be a top show winner, in 1903 Vidal pointed out that there was room for great improvement in the

Johnnie Fawe II was one of the excellent black Persians bred by Dr. Roper at the turn of the century in England and exported to the United States. He won top prizes all over the country. Breeders of blacks were rare at the time because of the obstacles they faced in obtaining the perfectly black coat. Roper achieved the best results when the sire was black, one of his parents black, and the queen tortoiseshell.

black cats. Many had a brown tinge and in some lights, it was possible to see tabby markings. By 1909, the black was considered not only popular, but really good specimens were seen at the shows. The color was felt to be most difficult to obtain and, interestingly enough, to maintain, as exposure to sun, rain, or ill health would spoil the coat's color. We cannot imagine any modern breeder whose black Persians would ever experience rain.

The blue Persians of 1903 were felt to be far more developed in regard to soundness of coat color than any other color of Persian. The lighter the shade of blue, the more difficult it was to obtain soundness and clarity of color. The beautiful cats of "...Northern India are constantly being stolen and taken across the Himalayas and the only cats that manage to survive the journey through the high, rare air of the passes are the blues," reported Vidal. He also reported that there were colonies of blues and blue tabbies in Russia that were able to survive the hard Russian winters.

Kew Iris bred by Dr. and Mrs. Ottolengui, won many top prizes in England and America and was considered one of the best blues ever bred in the early 1900s. Dr. Ottolengui became secretary of the Atlantic coast branch of the cat Fancy in 1902 and bred Persians in the fashionable summer community of Saratoga, New York.

The blue Persian was first exhibited at the Crystal Palace Show in London in 1871. These blue Persian cats were quite dark in color and were known as London Smokes. It was believed that a really good blue Persian was not difficult to produce. However, the emphasis was placed, even in 1909, on creating a coat of a pale, even shade of blue (which was called lavender blue and is still identified as such today). In England in 1901 The Blue Persian Cat Society was formed for the purpose of producing a blue Persian having a pale shade of lavender-blue coat and deep orange eye color. The pale-coated blues, however, had what today's breeders would describe as a pretty nondescript eye color, lemon-yellow. The dominance of the blue was such that by at least the 1950s, it was the color against which all others were judged. Blue Persians were so preeminent in type that they consistently took the bulk of Best-in-Show and Best Kitten awards.

In 1903, Vidal reported that there were some magnificent specimens of what were called orange cats. Today, this color is described as solid (or self) red. However, in 1903, all of these cats suffered from markings on the head and legs — much as with the silver Persians of the time. The brightest or deepest red color possible was preferred, as it is today. The problem in 1903 was that the cats which had the clearest-colored coats also had the lightest-colored eyes. Most were also marred by cream colored chins which was considered a great fault. The orange Persians in

A noted top-prize winner and stud of 1903 was Torrington Sunnysides, an orange or self-red. His coat color was exceptional, lacking the head markings which troubled many breeders. He sired several prize kittens which his breeder sent to America, where they "gained distinction over the water."

1909 were described as very beautiful cats without any tabby markings. This tendency toward tabby markings is, of course, still the challenge to any breeder working to perfect the self-red color; many of the solid red Persians do have vestigial tabby markings. However, it is the overall impression that a cat gives the judge which determines whether any red Persian's color is evaluated as solid red or red tabby.

Ch. Romaldkirk Admiral was one of a famous pair of cream Persians bred by Miss Beal, known as the "Heavenly Twins" in the 1903 cat Fancy. Admiral and his twin, Ch. Romaldkirk Midshipmate, were big boned, fawn in color, and in any season had excellent coats. Experts of the period said that no creams had yet been bred that could beat these twin cats in the show ring.

In 1903, A. Burland held that strides had been made in producing a pale, even shade of coat in the cream Persians. However, it was felt that many creams were really too dark and bordered on the color then identified as orange. By 1909, the cream was coupled with a darker shade referred to as fawn. The fawn was a shade or two darker than cream, but Persians of this color were considered the same color. The cream/fawn Persians were described as having (even in 1909) eye color of "...deep copper or brown color." Even though these cream and fawn Persians had the eye color we have come to prize in the Persian today, their type was described as being "... inclined to be long in the face, although a few of the best have been bred with snub faces." A large, handsome, even-colored fawn or cream was reported to have been much admired by the public. Fortunately, these early creams were able to pass their blazing copper eye color on to other Persian colors. It is, for example, the blazing eye color in the black Persian which creates a tremendous impact on any cat lover.

Fulmer Zaida was a champion silver, owned by Lady Decies in the early 1900s, shown here with a display of trophies won on the show bench. Zaida was considered the lightest and most perfect specimen of the color by the Fancy in 1903.

SHADED PERSIANS

The silver Persian was considered, from the outset of the cat Fancy in both Britain and America, just as it is today, one of the most beautiful colors of all. Burland points out in 1903 that, "...of late they have been rather inbred and do not often have the bone and substance of the Brown Tabbies." A pale lavender tint was one of the most preferred colors and there had not been a perfectly-colored silver Persian shown in that "... most of those shown have distinct markings on the head and legs." By 1909, the silver Persian was recognized as occurring in three distinct colors: the Chinchilla-silver Persian, the shaded-silver Persian, and the masked-silver Persian. The Chinchilla-silver was expected to be as "...pale a silver as possible, with little or no tabby marking or dark shading." Preferred were cats nearly self-silver-colored all over (a total absence of all tabby markings), with a distinct lavender hue that could only be detected by placing a pure colored lavender-tinted cat along side what was called a "dirty white" Chinchilla-silver. The Chinchilla-silver was required to be totally free of any brown or cream tinges. Many early silver Persians were considered to have the cream-tinge fault—a very serious fault indeed to those who evaluated the Chinchillas in 1909. The first shaded Persians were almost certainly a silver-colored variety that were produced in Great Britain in the early 1880s. The best-known of these silver varieties and the most lightly-shaded came to be known as the Chinchilla. By the turn of the century there were still very few good Chinchillas in either Britain or America. The genetic problem was inbreeding, which tended to weaken the strain. A suggested outcross was the shaded-silver Persian. In 1909, what many of today's silver breeders, particularly in the United States, consider to be the desirable practice of color-breeding silver Persians, that is breeding the Chinchilla-silver to the shaded-silver, was considered to be outcrossing.

Mrs. F. Champion, who founded the Silver Society in England in 1900, won the Best in Show award in New York in 1907 with this shaded-silver, Argent Glorious. Champion contributed much to improving the health and eye color of this color.

The 1909 version of the shaded-silver Persian was considered an indispensable color and was much admired for its type, size, wealth of coat, and coloring. Breeders found these shaded-silver Persians necessary for outcrossing with Chinchilla-silvers. Shaded-silvers were to be well-shaded in color, not too dark, but an even, bright shade. A "...dingy blue-gray color or any 'smutty' appearance" was to be avoided. Silver Persians are born with definite tabby markings; as they mature, the tabby markings diffuse as the coat lengthens creating the black tipping for which the color is noted. Just as it is today, there was difficulty in 1909 in differentiating between the Chinchilla and the shaded-silver: "There is really a great difference between a good Chinchilla Silver and a good Shaded Silver, but it is hard to distinguish between a dark Chinchilla and a light shaded silver." This could be a quote from one of today's judges some ninety years after

Ch. Lord Sylvester was considered the most perfect example of the masked silver, a variety no longer bred or shown. He was the greatest international winner shown at the time, winning many first prizes in England and New York in each year from 1902–1906.

this observation was made!

The masked silver Persian was shown in the early 1900s. In 1909 they were still considered to be a new variety and few were being bred. Most of the masked silvers that had been shown were considered to be spoiled smoke Persians. The ideal masked silver was described as being a very beautiful animal which "...in coloring , or...in marking,...should resemble the Siamese cat; that is to say, they should have a black mask or face, black feet, and legs. The body should be as pale a silver as possible, with neither a dark spine line nor tabby markings; the silver should be free from any cream or yellow, the eyes deep golden or orange." This striking color disappeared from the show bench. Perhaps it was because of the challenge of producing a tabby-free silver Persian with what we would probably consider to be black smoke points. Because they were of the orange-eyed family of cats, silver Persian breeders would have been reticent to introduce this color into their breeding programs. Dual problems would have been created: the muddying of the coat color on the Chinchilla or the shaded-silver and the disastrous effect on eye color which often occurs in using orange-eyed cats to breed with silver Persians.

The difficulty of introducing any other color into a silver Persian breeding program is well recognized. Muddy color, tabby markings, eye color other than the required green or blue-green of the silver Persian Standard—all make outcrossing to any copper-eyed (orange-eyed) cat a challenge. Breeders have discovered that outcrossing produces color problems. By the time the color problems have been eliminated in subsequent generations, the usual result is a loss of the type or feature that was the main purpose of the original outcross. However, there is always the chance that a breakthrough will occur. This is the challenge of breeding cats, and, in particular, the beautiful green or blue-green-eyed silver Persians.

Teufel, a black smoke bred in England by Mrs. Sinkins, won many first prizes and specials at shows in the early 1900s. Because of his unmarked black face, white undercoat, and excellent temperament, he was considered near-perfect.

SMOKE PERSIANS

The smoke Persian was first given its own breed classes in Great Britain in 1893. In 1903 the smoke Persian was a relatively new breed. There were not very many being shown. The cats were required to have "coal black" tips on the hairs which, "...when blown aside should be white." They also had a light ruff and ear feathers. Burland tells us that smokes are "...rather unsatisfactory as, when they change their coat, they often appear as bad blacks...." They were to have orange eyes.

By 1909, the smokes were valued as being one of the most beautiful varieties. "Their color is most effective, and there is no other animal exactly like it, the nearest, perhaps, being the marmoset monkey." The breeders were working to produce a Persian whose coloring was the same as today's black smoke Persian. The greatest emphasis was density of color: the head, face, and paws should appear black, with no trace of tabby markings. "The body should be as even in coloring as possible...." The roundness of the head was emphasized since it was felt that "...the mask shows up the shape of the face; and should it be long, it is double accentuated, giving a plain and faulty expression."

There are beautiful smoke Persians on the show bench today that truly appear to be solid blacks or blues, but which have a brilliant white undercoat. The cameo (red) smoke generally has exceptional type, but does not truly appear, as yet, to be a self-red cat. The chocolate and lilac smokes are still being developed. The chocolate-tortie and lilac-cream (described as lilac-tortie by the GCCF) have been granted championship status in America but have only received preliminary recognition from the GCCF.

Ch. Don Pedro of Thorpe, owned by Mrs. Slingsby, was a silver tabby bred in England, described as "...one of the most perfect cats ever exhibited."

Full recognition is given by the GCCF to tortie smokes in which the white undercoat is covered by tipping of black, red, and cream, well-broken in patches; cream smokes with a body color of cream shading to white on the flanks and sides, with the mask and feet cream in color; and blue-cream where the tipping consists of the colors blue and cream softly intermingled.

TABBY PERSIANS

The silver tabby Persian was considered a great challenge to the breeders in the early 1900s. Vidal states, "There is no greater opening for clever breeding than in Silver Tabbies." The cats being exhibited were not nearly "strong enough marked." The ground color had to be a very clear silver, "quite free from muddiness, with markings as black and clear as possible." The complaint was that some of the silver–tabby Persians being shown were lighter in color than Persians being shown in the silver class. By 1909, the silver-tabby Persian was still considered to be very rare; that is, there were very few good specimens being shown. The cat had to show "...clear wide black tabby markings on a pale silver ground color, the markings being as distinct as possible from the ground color; any blurring or ticking of the markings..." was considered a fault. The color had to be free of any cream or brown tint (a fault which today's tabby breeders refer to as tarnish which is still considered very undesirable.) The eye color was hazel or green. A good-silver tabby Persian continues to be rare today. Comparatively few are being shown. When a good example of the silver-tabby Persian is exhibited, it presents a spectacular study in contrast. This color continues to be a great challenge to breeders.

In 1903, Vidal mentions blue-tabby Persians as being exhibited in the United States but comments that this is "...simply another name for

Ch. Persimmon was a brown tabby owned by Frances Simpson, the chronicler of the early history of breeds and the cat Fancy. He had a round face, snub nose, tiny ears, and short tail, all considered perfect features. His markings, however, were too heavy and he had a white underlip, which did not stop him from winning top awards.

bad blues." The blue-tabby Persians of today are relatively rare in the Persian breed; however, with their overall warm, fawn patina and old-rose colored nose leather, these blue-pattern on pale-bluish-ivory-ground-colored cats are gorgeous to behold.

The brown tabby of 1909 received a great deal of attention in the United States. However, in 1903 they were considered rather common. It was pointed out that they did not have a light enough ground color; the ground color was supposed to be "...a golden brown and not the muddy color often seen." The markings were considered to be "...too thick and sometimes so much so as to almost extinguish the brown ground color." Another point was made in 1903 by A. Burland's stating that the "...cats should have orange or brown eyes, not green." White chins were very persistent and undesirable. It is also stated that brown tabbies could also be mackerel marked, "...a combination between spots and bars...even though the word tabby "really means striped." A detailed 1909 description of the cat stated that the ground color of the brown tabby should be of "...a rich tawny tint; this should be as even as possible extending to the extremities, especially the lips and chin, which are so often white shaded to dirty white; this latter fault has been hard to eradicate, but it has been done...." A great deal is mentioned about the pattern which is the same as the classic- or blotched-tabby pattern of today. Regarding conformation, brown tabbies were required to be "...heavy and thick in build and have large heads; they should have orange or golden eyes; the coat...is often inclined to be short and thick, but to be perfect, they should show as much quality as the Silvers or Blues." The principal points on which the breeders were

Ch. Topsy of Merevale bred in England by Mrs. Bignell was considered one of the top tortoiseshell specimens in the Fancy of 1903. It is hard to discern what was considered her fine coloring, for it was reported in 1903 that "...a tortoiseshell makes a terribly poor picture when reproduced in photography."

concentrating were breeding for "...soundness of chin...a deep fawn or cream, not nearly white, eye coloring, richness of ground color and distinctness of markings." However, the breeders were charged with not sacrificing shape and strength to achieve these ends. The tendency to white or off-white creamy chins has been almost eliminated from the brown tabby Persians exhibited today. While the ground-color may not be as rich as desired, the pattern and type are often outstanding.

The orange tabby or red tabby was judged to have produced far more good specimens in 1909 than had the brown tabby. Even though there were superior examples of the orange tabby, the solid orange cat was the more popular. For the orange tabby cats, the ground color was described as being a clear, light, orange, or sandy color which contrasted with the deep, rich, reddish-brown markings. As much contrast as possible was desired between the ground color and the markings. The chin and extremities tended to "...shade to a light or white," the chin was to be "...deep-colored right to the lips." Orange tabby cats were described in many cases as being "...long in face and high on leg."

PARTICOLOR PERSIANS

Tortoiseshell Persian cats of 1909 were felt to be "...peculiar in coloring, resembling a piece of tortoise-shell." The 1903 tortoiseshell Persian had colors which "... should be evenly distributed and well broken, viz., black, orange and yellow." Tabby markings were unacceptable. The tortoiseshell Persians were considered to be "...emblematic of Spain." By 1909, the color was described as being "...black, orange and cream patches...irregular in shape, but distinct in coloring, the more distinct and deeper in color the better; the head, ears, tail, and legs should also be patched with no trace of tabby markings visible."

BI-COLOR PERSIANS

The beautiful American calico Persian of today traces its beginnings to the early years of the cat Fancy in the United States. However, Burland relates in 1903 that in the tortoiseshell and white Persian "...the chest and nose were to be white with color on either cheek." This color combination is still referred to by purists who insist that true calico is basically a white cat with a colored, clearly-patched mantle which starts at the tip of the nose and continues over the top of the head, across the shoulders and back, continuing on to the end of the tail. We have also heard the opinion that the true calico Persian should look as if a patched cat had stepped

Peggy Primrose fits Harrison Weir's description of a good tortoiseshell-and-white. White coloring dominates the chest and belly; the color is layed on in patches; the face shows some uniformity of color; the nose is white; and the general coloring is rich and varied. Though dramatic in color, appearances of this color on the show bench were rare. The 1903 Westminster show in England had only one entry.

into a pail of milk producing a coat whose color is two-thirds white (on the underside of the cat) and one-third patched, with black-, red-, and cream-color on the top of the cat. Any other combination is considered to be tortoiseshell-and-white (except in the case of the van-calico in the United States which has all color confined to the extremities with one or two small spots of body-color. The remainder of the cat's body color must be white).

POINTED COLORS

This more recent color strain in the Persian was the result of cross-breeding between the Siamese and longhaired cats. After one attempt to mate these types by Swedish geneticists in 1924, two workers at the Harvard Medical School in the 1930s made a more determined and successful attempt to mate a Siamese with smoke, silver-tabby, and black Persians. One result of the experiments was the Debutante—the first pointed longhair produced in the United States in 1935. At the same time, in Great Britain, attempts at this type of cross-breeding were underway. It was not until the 1950s that this new breed was recognized in Great Britain where it is known as the colorpoint longhair and in the United States as the Himalayan. Of the North American registries only the CFA and the ACA have incorporated the Himalayan breed into the Persian category. The other associations regard the Himalayan as a separate breed.

TRADITIONAL VS MODERN TYPE

Within the past twenty-five years, a revolution in the look of the Persian cat has occurred. Led by the American show bench, Persian cats have been bred to produce a cat that closely approximates the Standard as it has been defined for many years. Producing a very snub-nosed Persian with large, round eyes, set in a round head with small ears; a heavy-boned, short-legged, cobby body; with a luxurious coat has been the aim of breeders in the United States for many, many years.

It is the head type more than any other point, which has separated the American from the English cat Fancy. Where the British breeders have worked to produce exquisite color and a luxurious, long, flowing coat, the American breeders have worked to add the dimension of extreme type to these other important factors. American cats are described by British cat Fanciers as "over-typed". In the view of most of today's British judges, the Persian noses have become too short and the features have been selectively bred to produce a snub-nosed cat that appears to have a *retroussé* nose when viewed in profile. Modern type cats are appearing everywhere in the cat world today. British breeders have produced cats which, while not generally acceptable to the show bench sanctioned by GCCF, are being exported to other areas for breeding programs. Australia, an area where breeders have produced marvelous, long, coats and beautiful color, is currently producing Persian cats with the modern type using, in some cases, the cats imported from Great Britain that are deemed "over–typed" on the GCCF show bench.

HOW MUCH IS TOO MUCH ?

There is great controversy regarding the modern type Persian which is seen often not only on the American show bench, but is sometimes seen on the show bench of other countries. The main controversy concerns the overall health and stamina of the very extreme, modern type Persians. Many hold the opinion that these cats are not healthy; that such cats cannot properly breathe or eat, in the most extreme cases, because of the shortness of the head. We first heard these arguments nearly thirty-five years ago. There have always been those who decry the apparent poor health of the modern type Persians. In Paris, France, in 1988, Will Thompson was questioned by the press about the very high-style Persians that they were calling American-type Persians. During the interview, he coined the term modern type as opposed to the term traditional type which refers to the older, more moderate style of Persian cats.

Since the genes that were carefully selected by Persian breeders to produce the short nosed Persians of today were present in the cats originally imported into the United States from Great Britain and Europe, it is difficult to determine in actuality whether today's Persian belongs to any single area or country. What breeders have actually produced are Persian cats whose head and appearance fits the Standard as described in the 1909 book by D. B. Champion, *Everybody's Cat Book*. While it is true that these very extreme cats are quite common on the American show bench, more and more breeders world-wide are becoming eager to own one of these modern type Persians.

We have been told that this style of Persian has been produced by cat breeders in Great Britain from their bloodlines; however, GCCF judges are opposed to this style of cat. The GCCF, guided by their veterinary sub-committee, is concerned that recognition of a modern type Persian may result in the production of cats with severe health problems. Reference to, and disapproval of extreme type, is implied in the GCCF Standard list of withholding faults. As such, these over typed Persians are finding their way to other parts of the world where they are accepted and used in increasing numbers of breeding programs. This is an example of the judges in an area having the effect of determining the overall style, type, and appearance of cats. The GCCF judges prefer the distinctly, more moderate style of the traditional-type Persian, whereas some members of the cat Fancy in the rest of the world appear to prefer the more extreme modern type Persian.

Which is right? Since this is an area of subjective evaluation of all the factors that embody the Persian cat, only the cat's human companions can really decide. People will acquire the type and style of companion cat which appeals to them. The feline judge serves as critic and arbiter of that which is defined as being in good taste in the subjective area of beauty as defined by the Persian Standard. Of course, this area includes not only appearance, but also health, and what we term the "companion-ship index." The companionship index evaluates the animal's ability to bond with human companions producing a true partnership wherein each contributes to the happiness and well-being of the other. In the end, the cat owner desires a beautiful, healthy animal which rates high on the compan-ionship index so that the cat will bond with his human companion produc-ing that state of comfort which only affection and need can fulfill—on both sides of the companionship equation.

The Persian with its gentle and affectionate temperament is an ideal family pet.

CHAPTER III

HOW TO CHOOSE AND CARE FOR YOUR PERSIAN

Human life is more focused in urban centers than in any other period in history. Sharing our homes with pets has become a problem because of the pace and demands of urban living. Because the cat is so easy to live with, it has become our most popular animal companion. From the garden cats of England, to the moggies of Australia, and the household companion cats of the Americas, the feline reigns supreme in the area of hearth and home.

There are many ways in which to obtain a cat. A friend whose cat has had kittens is often very pleased to provide a kitten from the litter. Many people go to animal shelters to rescue cats without homes. Others use word-of-mouth, magazines, or pet shops. Most cat breeders prefer not to use pet shops because of the inability of many pet shop owners to

A playful and boisterous Persian kitten will give you many hours of pleasure.

provide proper, knowledgeable kitten care. Pet shop proprietors, however, often can refer a prospective cat owner to ethical breeders in the local area. In our opinion, the best source for a beautiful cat or kitten is from an ethical breeder. The question is, just how does the prospective cat owner find these breeders? This is not as difficult as many would suspect. However, prior to this major step, there are other very important matters to be considered and important steps to be taken.

THE FIRST STEP

The first step is to realize that acquiring a cat is a long term responsibility. Too often people begin with the idea that getting a cat will be fun for them and their children, and the cat will provide a great opportunity to teach the children the facts of life by letting the cat have just one litter of kittens.

While owning a cat may prove to be fun, using a cat as a lesson in life is generally a definite mistake. In fact, most ethical breeders will not allow one of their cats or kittens to go to any home where having a litter or two for the children's education is a stated purpose. The reason is that there are important responsibilities involved in acquiring a cat which many people may not realize, such as immunization shots, training, and responsible placement of the kittens in good homes. Generally the expense and the necessity of finding responsible homes for each and every kitten is overlooked.

How many times have you seen children standing near a market with a box labeled, "free kittens," or noticed the free kitten ads in the newspapers and on the community bulletin boards in libraries and supermarkets? And more unfortunately, have you ever visited a local animal shelter and found cats, kittens, and mother cats with new kittens that have been abandoned? The responsibilities involved in owning a cat should not be taken lightly.

A LIFETIME RESPONSIBILITY

The acceptance of a cat or kitten into the family circle is an agreement to share your home with your cat companion for a lifetime. A cat's life span is far shorter than that of humans. A Persian may live to be ten to twelve years old; however, there have been cases where Persians have lived to the age of twenty or more. Nonetheless, bringing a cat into your home requires a commitment that you will be responsible for the care of that animal for life. Many times we have met people who feel they just have to part company with their cat because they are moving into an apartment where the landlord will not permit pets. In these cases, our opinion is that the owner should not move into a pet-free apartment or house. Owning a cat is not a simple matter of convenience, it is an obligation to the cat.

A HOME FOR YOUR CAT

The second step is to realize that your home will have to be cat-proofed for the safety of your new companion. Many people do not stop to consider that their lifestyles will have to be modified to provide for the cat's needs and safety. Removal of poisonous house plants, checking for chemicals that are used for rodent or insect control, elimination of escape routes that will permit the cat to wander resulting in dangers from cars, catnappers who sell animals to testing laboratories, or to unthinking people who will harm your Persian, are all precautions to be taken before the arrival of your new companion. The need to adjust your thinking to allow for cat hair, cat litter trays, grooming, and feeding is something to consider seriously for each will be a part of your life and a necessity for your cat companion. Remember, you will be sharing your home with your Persian.

WHICH CAT FOR YOUR HOME?

There is another very important decision that must be made, and that is to determine exactly which of the beautiful cats to choose to bring into your home. There are a multitude of colors and breeds. If you have made the decision to acquire a Persian, you must carefully consider the fact that Persian cats have long, flowing coats. This, of course, means that you must be willing to groom your cat daily, and to cope with the long-hair that the cat will shed onto your furniture, your bed, your rugs, and everyone's lap. There is no way to avoid this shedding coat. It is as natural as rain and sunshine. If you have concerns about owning a Persian due to the longhair problem, it would be a good idea to talk with owners of these cats.

The daily grooming that is very necessary for a Persian will become a ritual for you and your companion cat. Generally, grooming your Persian will only require a few minutes of your time unless the cat has managed to get a tangle or mat in the coat. To remove the mat without damage to the rest of the coat or without hurting the cat requires a little more time.

WHICH IS WHICH?

The decision to share your home with a Persian is only one of the many decisions you have to make. You also must decide which is more suitable for you: an adult cat or a kitten, a male or a female, a whole cat or a neutered cat. Each of these considerations is as important as your initial decision to acquire a Persian.

Most people generally think of a kitten when they decide to share their home with a cat. However, there is another alternative. You can acquire an adult cat that is more settled in its ways and not quite so rambunctious. This would be a good choice for a home in which life is very busy, or for older adults who do not relish the idea of dealing with the playful and boisterous antics of a kitten. There is a school of thought that holds that if a cat has any tendency towards undesirable traits (such as forgetting house training, chewing on clothing or shoes, or a tendency to bite or scratch) these will be apparent in the young adult. It is easier to identify signs of a psychologically maladjusted animal in an older cat.

If you are lucky enough to be offered the opportunity to share your home with a prize-winning Persian that the breeder wishes to place in a good home, this might be another consideration. While not readily available, there are those special cats placed in good homes from time-to-time by responsible breeders. These cats can provide some advantages. They are generally outstanding examples of their Persian color and pattern and will often have the title of Champion or Grand Champion attached to their pedigree. (This, of course, adds nothing to the cat, but can add a little excitement and pride to the home in which the cat lives.) These cats are

A little excitement and much pride can be added to the home which acquires a show-quality Persian or one that has retired.

usually already neutered or spayed. You will not have to bear the expense of these veterinary procedures nor the convalescent stage following them. Additionally these cats are fully mature so that there is no question about their adult appearance.

One disadvantage of adopting an adult cat is that you will miss the enjoyment of seeing your Persian mature. You will also have to be more patient with the older cat in that you will have to work to provide emotional security for the animal. It may take a longer period of time for a mature adult than for a kitten to feel secure and a part of the family. Loud noises and rapid, threatening movements must be avoided with the older cat until

This Victorian cat house could serve as a useful model for an enclosed protection in which your cat can enjoy the out-of-doors.

security is well-established. You must keep close control over your adult cat's movements. If you allow the cat freedom out-of-doors, a confused, older cat may try to return to a former home. We have all heard stories of cats who have found their way back home or to their former owner's new home over hundreds, and even thousands of miles of difficult terrain, bad weather, and other hazards. It is not a good idea to allow a cat outside without providing a safe, enclosed area, or personal supervision, so as to avoid the hazards of the urban environment. This is even more important for the newly-acquired adult cat which will be somewhat confused by its displacement.

The male cat is usually larger and will be more muscular and robust. Unless you plan to do a great deal of study and enter the world of breeding pedigreed Persians, it is best to have your young Persian neutered between the ages of six and eight months, depending upon the sexual development of the individual animal. Some are ready for altering earlier than six months of age. If you are not prepared to have your family vet perform this simple procedure, you must be prepared to deal with one of nature's little surprises.

Most adult male cats will carefully, but completely lay claim to their territory by scent-marking the boundaries of their territories. This practice is known as spraying. Your Persian will suddenly become the champion sprayer of all time, wandering about the house, lifting his tail, and with rapid back and forth movements signal that he is about to produce an acrid, highly odorous liquid known as cat spray. It will permeate the area, announcing unpleasantly to all that this place belongs to your Persian. It also serves to advertise his presence to all the female cats in the area. If a non-neutered male cat happens to get outside by himself, he will fight with other males for territorial dominance and the right to breed with any females in season in the area. These are not pleasant experiences. This adult, male behavior is a natural and expected pattern of behavior from any adult, male Persian.

The solution, of course, is to neuter your cat before this behavior occurs. You will quickly agree to neuter your male Persian if you have had the unhappy experience of having to take your beautiful Persian male to the family vet to be patched up after a major cat fight with another tom in the area. Torn ears, injured eyes, bites, and abscessed, clawed areas are common.

There is no reason for any cat odor in your house (unless you allow a whole male cat to wander about the house). Cats love to be clean and to live in a clean environment. However, the spraying male cat presents a formidable challenge to control unwanted odors even for the most fastidious home owner.

THE FEMALE PERSIAN

Generally, the female Persian is smaller in overall size than her male counterpart. Female Persians have the same beautiful, long hair and general conformation or physical appearance as the male. However, the female presents a challenge of a very different nature. If the female is not neutered she will soon erupt into a veritable volcano of strange screeches, yowls, and howls known as calling. From the very top of her lungs she will announce to the entire world that she has suddenly realized she has the ability and responsibility to become a mother. The screeching is accompanied by increased agitation and a characteristic mating posture. The female will kneel on her front legs, raise her hindquarters, curve her spine, tread, and present her most private parts to all and sundry. This fertility rite will continue for anywhere from one to four, six, or even ten days. This behavior will occur several times in a regular cycle accompanied by efforts to escape from captivity. If your female manages to escape, you can rest assured that sixty-three to sixty-nine days later she will present you with a litter of kittens, and not all necessarily from the same father. You will then have the responsibility for finding suitable homes for these new kittens of mixed and unknown ancestry.

Of course, all of this can be avoided by a trip to your family vet. The procedure is called spaying and is a well-studied surgical procedure. Some vets now perform this operation using a very minor incision into the cat's internal structure. After the procedure your female will no longer call and seek mates. Another important reason for having your female Persian altered is to avoid health problems. If a female cat is allowed to call over and over again without being mated, her physical health may be in jeopardy. Physical problems such as cystic ovaries can occur.

Many people resist the idea of spaying and neutering their cats. They argue that people should allow nature to take its course. They believe that it is not natural to deny animals the right to reproduce. Many believe altered cats become fat and lazy. However, reason will show that only the most responsible and knowledgeable breeders have the ability and patience to cope with the problems presented by an entire cat. Not only is there the problem of dealing with the spraying male or calling female, but there is also the problem of dealing with the important responsibility of finding *suitable* homes for all of the kittens produced.

Breeding and selling pedigreed cats is *not a lucrative business* even if you are selling Persians. Even though you might have paid a very good price to acquire your own Persian, remember that the breeder has underwritten all the expenses of establishing a bloodline of pedigreed Persians and has financed all of the costs associated with owning, breeding, showing, and maintaining a cattery (a group of breeding cats). We know of very few people who have Persian catteries who do much more than just break even in their endeavor. One quickly learns that breeding cats is a labor of love, not of financial reward.

THE NEXT STEP

Having considered whether you prefer a cat or a kitten, a male or female, entire or neutered or spayed, you will make your choice. Whatever your choice, you are about to enter the world of cat ownership. It is a world that can be satisfying, amusing, warm, and very special. The next important step is to select exactly which color and pattern Persian will be your special companion.

There is a rainbow of coat colors and patterns available in the Persian palette. Each has a special look and appeal. The problem for the new owner is not which to choose, but rather which not to choose. With such variety available, it is not easy to select the cat that will be with you for many happy years. No matter how many thousands of Persian cats we see, handle, and judge around the world, we have yet to see one that we did not consider a work of art. The problem has always been that we want at least one of each. This, of course, is not within the realm of good sense or reality. If you consider that there are at least 141 colors and patterns of Persian cats recognized for championship competition by FIFe, the Feline International Federation, you can appreciate the problem a potential Persian buyer faces in making a selection. This does not take into account that there are also colors and patterns that are not recognized for the championship show bench.

WHERE TO BEGIN

The best place to begin searching for the Persian cat of your dreams is at a cat show or cat exhibition. Nearly every weekend in the United States, the United Kingdom, and nearly as often in Europe, you will find that there is at least one cat show being held. They range from small, one-day affairs to the giant shows in England where two to three thousand cats compete on the day of the show. The largest cat show in the world is the National Cat Show held in London in December of each year. At this prestigious exhibition you can see most colors and patterns of every breed in competition for championships, grand championships, and many other important prizes and awards.

Also in Great Britain, one of the most important events in the

The National Cat Club holds its championship show in London every year in December. It is the largest cat show in the world where most colors and patterns of all breeds and varieties may be seen.

show season is the Supreme Cat Show held in December at the National Exhibition Centre. Every cat exhibit at this huge show must have already won awards at other championship shows held around the country in order to qualify for entry in this event. Here, a large selection of Persians can be found. There is a national show held by the clubs in Australia as well as a World Show organized by FIFe each year in a different member country. Exhibits in this show must have won previous awards to qualify for entry.

In the United States, regional shows are hosted by most of the major cat organizations at which cats, kittens, and altered cats compete to qualify for the top awards all over the country. It is at these shows that the largest selection of Persians can be seen.

AT THEIR MOST BEAUTIFUL BEST

Most shows, if they are two-day events, are held on Saturday and Sunday. Sometimes, they are held in conjunction with a holiday and may be on any day of the week on which the holiday falls. Once you have located the cat shows that you can attend, plan to go early on the first day of the show. This is generally when the smallest number of spectators attends. You should note that shows in England are traditionally only held on a Saturday. With fewer people around, you have a better chance to get a copy of the show catalog that lists the name, color, breeder, and owner of every cat in competition. A catalog can be purchased as you enter the show hall. With this guide in hand, you can then leisurely stroll up and down the rows of cages looking carefully at each of the cats in the show.

In the United States, the cages are usually carefully decorated to offer a backdrop for displaying the color and coat of each cat exhibited. The cage displays are carefully decorated with colors and textures selected to set off the best features of each breed and color. For example, black Persians are generally not exhibited in cages with a black color scheme. These luxurious surroundings show the cats at their very best by contrasting and complementing the cats' coat color and pattern.

Judging and exhibition requirements around the world differ according to rules and regulations set down by the various countries' governing federations. In the United Kingdom and other parts of the Commonwealth having rules based on GCCF practices, all exhibits to be judged must be in cages bearing no distinguishing features. The base of the cage must be lined with a plain white blanket for the cat's comfort. A plain white feeding dish and water bowl are allowed.

Exhibitors will sometimes show a famous or well-known cat which is probably already a champion or a grand champion, as a form of advertisement for their bloodlines. These exhibitors are no longer interested in having the cat judged and will pay for an "exhibition cage" which can be decorated with curtains, cushions or anything else to make it look attractive. Rosettes and prize cards won at other shows will probably be displayed and perhaps a copy of the cat's pedigree.

In Europe, Scandinavia, and other parts of the world not following GCCF guidelines, exhibits are usually brought by stewards from their cages to a judging area. Since the judges will not see the cages until they have finished judging, it is permissible for the cages to be decorated and to bear distinguishing marks. This probably makes the entire show much more interesting for those members of the visiting public who know little or nothing about cats.

At any cat show an attempt is made to exhibit each cat in top condition. Each cat is groomed to perfection for the show so it is a good opportunity to see the various breeds looking their very best. Each cage will display a number that corresponds to the numbered listings in the show catalog. In addition to the animal's name, the specific breed, color, pattern, name of sire, name of dam, name of breeder, and name of owner, will be listed in the catalog for each entry in the show.

To buy a Persian your attention should be focused on the "for sale" exhibits, as they may contain just the Persian you want. Be sure to visit all the Persian cat and kitten entries in the show. This will provide you with a large range of Persian colors and patterns to consider. Many breeders will want to take time for serious discussion with you about your plans for any cat or kitten they may sell you. Such arrangements are often made at a later date and by specific appointment. Often the breeder will have a business card which you may have so that you can easily contact them later when you are ready for your new Persian or when the breeder has kittens or cats available. Take the opportunity to discuss the fine points of each color and pattern of Persian, in which you have an interest, with the breeder of any example you see at the show. In the United States, when they are not engaged in giving their cat a last minute grooming for an upcoming trip to the judging ring, breeders are usually delighted to discuss the advantages offered by their color and pattern of Persian. In fact, you may find that a breeder may have kittens available in the near future.

Although there is no specific ruling from the GCCF in Great Britain, the practice of selling exhibits at a show is not encouraged. Many show managers will not permit "for sale" notices to be placed on the cages. However, you will still have every opportunity to talk to breeders and exhibitors whose cats and kittens particularly appeal to you. Arrangements for the subsequent purchase of a cat from the exhibitor's home can easily be made.

You will also be able to see Persians ranging from four months in age to mature specimens, providing you an opportunity to see how your kitten of choice may appear at maturity. Kittens are a pleasure to see, to hold, to pet, and to own, and they soon mature into beautiful, adult cats. But, the regal Persian adult is a very special pet to own.

NARROWING THE CANDIDATES

You may find that having seen many colors and patterns of Persians, you are thoroughly confused. Narrowing down the candidates can be made easier if you make a few preliminary decisions. First, decide whether you want a show-type Persian cat or if you would be equally pleased to own a more moderate example of the breed. A show-type Persian will be expensive, and the breeder will usually sell such a Persian only to someone who plans to exhibit the cat and work with the breeder of the cat to produce kittens—potentially better examples of the breed. These cats are not readily available as they usually represent the best that the breeder has produced for showing and exhibiting. Breeders continually strive to improve the breed. Show-type kittens generally represent the breeder's current best effort to produce cats that are close to the perfection

> 'THE VICARAGE, SANDAL MAYNER,
> NEAR WAKEFIELD,
> *October 14th*, 1882.
>
> ' *To* Mrs. VALLANCE.
>
> 'MADAM,—The kitten I have to sell is quite pure bred. The mother I bought for £1 1s. when quite a kitten from prize parents. The father is one we bred partly from Mrs. Radford's breed and partly from a splendid tom cat that was found living wild at Babbicombe, and that we had in our possession for some months, but unfortunately he is lost again now—I am afraid permanently. I think this kitten promises to be very like the mother. She is very handsome and has good points—brush, ear tips, and so on—but I consider her rather small. But the kitten may be finer, as the father is a large cat. Miss Grant's are related to ours on the father's side, but Mrs. Radford's very distantly, if at all.
>
> ' I do not think these Angora kittens are delicate. We have never failed in rearing them. The more new milk they have, and the better feeding, the finer cats they are likely to make. We do not have much trouble in keeping ours at home, as we live some distance from the village. We always give ours their principal meal at 6 p.m., and keep them shut up in a hay-loft until next morning. If you have a box wherever the kitten lives, with sifted sand or cinders in it, kept in a corner, you will find that the best way to ensure habits of cleanliness. If I hear nothing from you to the contrary I will send the kitten on Wednesday morning, 19th, by the early train from Derby station; and if you are not satisfied with the kitten I am willing for it to be returned within a day or two, if the return journey is paid and I am let know beforehand when to expect it.
>
> ' I remain, yours truly,
> 'GRACE HURT.'

A sales transaction recorded in this 1882 letter in which a kitten was sent on approval. Mrs. Vallance did buy the kitten, who grew to become one of the top-winning Chinchillas, Chinnie, found in the pedigrees of every breeder of this variety at the turn of the century in England. The asking price today would be $1.50.

outlined in the breed Standard.

The less high-style kittens represent those animals which breeders term pet-type examples of the Persian breed. This category of Persian will have the same ancestry, the same color, the same coat, and the same general appearance as their higher-priced show-type siblings. They may not have quite such a snubbed-nose, or as deep a nose break, the eyes may not be quite as round or deep in color, or they may have a slight coat color fault. These minor faults are important only in the show ring where every flaw, no matter how minor, is considered in selecting the cats for awards. To anyone who wants a beautiful Persian cat, but is not interested in showing, these minor flaws are of little importance. However, the difference in price between a show-type Persian and a pet-type Persian is important and is usually sizable. It is difficult to be precise about costs around the world.

So very much depends on the prosperity and income-levels of the different countries, and prices are, of course, always distorted by inflation, which varies from country to country. Of course, if you purchase your Persian kitten from one of the famous and successful breeders whose stock is highly sought, you may expect to pay a higher price than if you purchase your Persian from a breeder who has less experience in the breed.

The sleeping box in the Victorian cattery of Lady Decies who was a member of the committee of The National Cat Club. Much of her country house was dedicated exclusively to her longhair and shorthair cats. The cats' beds were specially designed by Lady Decies and the walls of the cats' rooms were adorned with pictures by Louis Wain, the most famous cat illustrator of his day.

Even so, breeders most often feel pleased if they are able to pay their expenses with the money they receive from sales. What may seem to be expensive to the new Persian buyer is, in fact, a bargain when all expenses that accrued in producing the kitten or cat in question are considered. Pet-type cats are usually sold with the understanding that the cat will be neutered or spayed. Most breeders will then provide the registration papers upon proof that the cat has been neutered or spayed unless they require that the cat never be shown at cat shows. In any event, in the United States, registration papers are made available after payment of an added fee ranging from $75.00 to $150.00 or more. In the United Kingdom registration papers are provided as required under the rules of the GCCF without any extra payment.

There is a third category of cat which is termed "breeder-quality". This category consists of kittens and cats that the breeder wishes others to continue working with to help improve the breed. These cats generally become part of a serious breeding program. They have no major or disqualifying faults and have a bloodline which indicates that they will produce a better-quality cat than they are themselves when they are properly bred.

Animals in this category are generally sold with the cat's registration papers included in the purchase price. Unless you intend to get involved in the world of pedigreed cats, purchasing a breeder-quality cat for one or two litters, based on the idea that you will help pay the expenses of buying and owning your own cat, is *not* a *good* idea. As stated earlier, *few breeders achieve a break-even position in breeding cats.* The economic considerations more than suggest that breeding cats is not a way to make money.

Once you have made your decision regarding the category of Persian you want, you have narrowed the field. Next, consider pattern. There are several patterns in the Persian spectrum. Mackerel tabbies have a pattern which includes narrow pencilings that run perpendicular to a line down the middle of the back, spotted tabbies have a pattern which consists of spots of color on a contrasting ground, and classic or blotched tabbies have a pattern that includes a definite bull's eye on each side of the body. (Only the classic pattern is recognized in Great Britain.) All of the tabby-patterned cats have bracelets, necklaces, vest buttons, rings on the tail, and an intricate letter M on the forehead as part of their complex patterns. They exist in several color combinations. Additionally, in the United States and FIFe there are patched tabbies. These are tabby cats, almost always female, whose pattern and color includes patches of red and/or cream overlaying their distinct tabby pattern. In Great Britain these are described as tortie tabbies.

Bi-color, and tabby-and-white Persians have a spectacular inverted V blaze of white centered on their faces, and white under the body. These cats appear to be wearing a tuxedo and exist in several solid colors-with-white and tabby-with-white combinations. Pointed cats are particularly beautiful and spectacular. The points are the facial mask, ears, feet, and tail. On a pointed cat, the body will generally be a pale, light color; and the points will be a totally different color providing a striking contrast. These are known as colorpoints by the GCCF in Great Britain. Patched cats which include calico, tortoiseshell, and blue-cream are multicolored

64

cats. Generally these are females, and in the United States it is preferred that the coat consists of distinct color patches. The GCCF in Great Britain requires a softly intermingled mix of two colors for blue-creams with no solid patches. These patterned Persians are a delight to behold. Their patterns present a striking appearance of complexity and beauty. However, not all people like the patterned or multi-colored Persians. If pattern is something you do not prefer, your search for your perfect Persian has narrowed once again; there are other equally beautiful alternatives.

For those whose concept of beauty accentuates simplicity, the solid or shaded Persian cat might be the choice. Solid-color Persians are available in several single-color coats. The tipped cat has a coat in which the tipping of color varies from a mere sprinkling of color to a generous dusting of color. An excellent example has tipping that is so complete that the coat appears to be one solid color because of the amount and depth of tipping on each hair shaft. However, when this deeply-tipped Persian's coat is separated , the coat reveals a contrasting undercoat color. There are tipped Persians in several colors, including some with multi-colored tipping. The black smoke Persian appears to be a black cat, but when the coat is parted, a stark white undercoat is revealed making the black smoke one of the most spectacular of all Persian colors and patterns.

THE PERSIAN COLOR PALETTE

The remaining criterion for your selection is the color that you find most appealing. If you select a multi-colored cat, your choice is limited to the colors that appear in that spectrum. Similarly, your choice from among the tabby, solid-color, pointed, bi-color, or tipped cats is limited only by the Persian palette itself. There are no greens, bright yellows, or sky blues in cat coat colors. There are whites, blacks, blues (gray-colored cats who at their best appear to be a pale lavender-blue shade), reds, creams (fawn), chocolates, and lilacs. In the pointed Persians there are also seal-points, chocolate-points, blue-points, lilac-points, flames (red), cream-points, blue-cream-points, chocolate-cream-points, several different colors of lynx points, as well as chocolate-tortie and lilac-cream-points. Beyond these colors and combinations of these colors and their dilutions and combinations, no others are available in the United States.

In Great Britain, the descriptive range for colorpoint cats is fairly wide. You may choose from solid-points, i.e., seal, blue, chocolate, lilac, red, and cream, or from tortie-points of seal, blue-cream, chocolate, or lilac-cream. For tabby-points, you may select from a palette of seal, blue, chocolate, lilac, red, or cream. Finally, you may choose from a combination of patterns of colorings described by the GCCF as tortie-tabby-point colors. They appear in just four color descriptions: seal-tortie-tabby, blue-cream-tabby, chocolate-tortie-tabby, and lilac-cream-tabby. This is a fairly bewildering array of color and pattern.

When deciding the color of the Persian we suggest you choose a color you consider beautiful. Your Persian's attitudes, moods, and antics will eventually be as important to you, if not more so, than your cat's color or pattern. Nevertheless, it is satisfying to select a Persian which meets your own idea of beauty. Whatever most pleases you and fills your need for beauty and companionship is the central issue when choosing your Persian. Your Persian will be your companion over a period of many years, and it cannot be exchanged, repainted, redecorated, or modified. The color will not change beyond the subtle changes which accompany maturity and the seasons of the year. The cat's appearance will only become more mature and expressive of the Persian type of head, body, and coat as your cat gets older. These are the basics which do not truly change through the years.

ACQUIRING YOUR PERSIAN

Having visited a cat show, you will have seen examples of the Persian you'd prefer to acquire. Hopefully, you will have established contact with one or more breeders of the type of cat you desire. We can suggest several ways to enable you to contact a breeder who will work with you to find the Persian you have in mind. There are several cat magazines published which carry breeder's listings. You can also contact the registering associations directly for their help in locating breeders in your general area. The GCCF publishes lists of breed club secretaries who will be happy to give you help.

WHAT YOU CAN EXPECT

Working with an ethical breeder to obtain your Persian carries many advantages. You will be given a guarantee of the cat's health for a limited period of time and be guaranteed that the cat has had all necessary preventive shots. Additionally the breeder will guarantee that the cat is physically sound in general. This, however, does not guarantee the cat from suffering a heart attack or some other health problem one day. The breeder will also document that the cat is as represented with a distinct bloodline or pedigree. The breeder will recommend a diet and, if required, the name of a reliable vet and will provide you with a wealth of knowledge regarding your chosen Persian cat including a pedigree. These are important points to a new cat owner. Where do you go if you encounter some problem which concerns you with respect to your new cat? There is no better place than contacting the breeder from whom you purchased the cat.

Most cat breeders are vitally concerned with the welfare of every cat they produce. They want the assurance that the cat is receiving proper treatment and that the home the cat lives in is the best home for that cat. Not all breeders will sell or place cats with everyone. If the breeder feels that the person or the prospective home is not good for the cat, they will not sell *or* give a cat to them.

When acquiring a new Persian, or cat of any breed, it's important to pre-pare your home and do a bit of "baby-proofing" since kittens in particular will find a way to get into everything.

CHAPTER IV

PREPARING FOR YOUR NEW PERSIAN

Now that you have selected your Persian and have found the perfect cat or kitten for your family, the next step is to prepare your home to receive and maintain your new companion. This is like baby-proofing a house. Your Persian will be filled with the desire to explore, smell, taste, and touch everything in your house. Eventually, your cat will find a way though every door, into every closet, cupboard, or drawer. You have a responsibility to search out and eliminate any potential hazard that might cause unhappy results.

A few of the more obvious but often overlooked hazards include open windows and doors, washing machines, dish washers, clothes dryers, rubber bands, cellophane or clear plastic film, needles attached to thread (cats swallow them), metal wrappers from food items which may catch your cat's tasty attention, or loose electrical cords that invite play. Anything an exterminator may have left as bait should be removed. Most exterminators have methods which will accomplish needed work without endangering the cat. However, you must tell them that you have a cat. There are other potential danger items or spots which you will be able to identify if you spend a few minutes in each room looking for them. You must inspect each room for possible problems and make the house completely cat-friendly.

IT MAY BE DEADLY

Any poisonous substances must be stored in areas that are cat-proof. Cupboards for storage should have latches or locks that even the most clever cat cannot open. There are many household supplies which are poisonous to cats. Be very careful in your choice of cleaning materials, as phenol-based compounds, for example, are poisonous to cats. The rule of thumb to keep in mind is that cats wash and groom themselves. Any residual material from house-cleaning products picked up on your cat's paws or coat will end up inside the cat. When a cat licks paws and coat as a normal part of regular grooming, any material walked through or lain on will be ingested by your cat.

PLANTS MAY BE POISONOUS

Take care with the plants in and around your house. Some are very poisonous to cats. For example, the philodendron contains calcium oxalate and will cause trauma which in extreme cases will produce total blockage of the windpipe due to swelling. This can result in a cat's death. Other plants to avoid are caladium, Christmas cherry, foliage from daffodils, delphinium, dieffenbachia, foxglove, holly, foliage from hyacinths, ivys, laurel, mistletoe, oleander, rhododendron, yew and some of the items found in dried arrangements including some seed pods and materials from tropical plants. If you have a question about any plant either indoors or outdoors, consult your local library for books about poisonous plants.

A SPECIAL PLACE

From the beginning, select a special place which your Persian can consider his or her own. Even if you decide to allow your Persian to sleep on your bed, it is necessary to establish a place which is solely for your cat. This should be a warm place which is free of drafts. The cat's bed should be placed in this special area. For your cat's sake, please don't put the bed in the same area as the litter tray. This is the same as someone putting your bed in your bathroom.

The cat bed should be large enough so that your Persian (kitten or adult) can turn around easily within the bed's confines. Most cats prefer an enclosed bed where they can feel safe and secure from challenge. A basket or compartment which is enclosed on at least three sides is perfect. A tent-like, enclosed compartment or a solid, lined box sturdy enough to support the weight of a cat that chooses to pounce on top of it are better yet. There are many different kinds of beds available, made of many materials, and available in most shops. Those that have a removable, washable lining which is replaceable are the best solution. Old baby blankets make wonderful bed liners for your cat. And, don't forget that your Persian cat will leave longhair in and on bedding, so choose materials for your own bed that are easy to keep clean and somewhat free of hair.

Your cat's bed is very important for feelings of security and general well-being. When all else fails, the bed will be a haven when the cat wishes to be alone, or needs to recharge those feline batteries, just as people need to do from time to time. A few minutes in the safety and security of a private place will do wonders.

THE LITTER TRAY

Your cat will require an indoor toilet facility or litter tray. This should consist of a non-porous tray large enough for your cat to turn around comfortably as a kitten or adult cat. Restaurant supply shops sell heavy plastic restaurant bussing trays (generally used to carry off soiled dishes) which are excellent for use as litter trays. They are usually a medium-gray or black, manufactured from a heavy, scratch-resistant, plastic compound, and are of sufficient height to keep the cat litter contained within. These trays are relatively inexpensive and very strong. They can be easily cleaned since they are designed with no nooks and crannies, or angled corners, and they stand up well to being sterilized with bleach or other good disinfectant. It is best to have at least two of these trays so that you can have one tray for your Persian to use while the other is being cleaned and prepared for use whenever a change of the litter tray is necessary.

By nature, the Persian is a very clean companion animal. By keeping the litter tray clean and free of debris and moisture at all times, you will be reinforcing your cat's natural desire to maintain his pristine cleanliness. Some Persians like to "swim" in the litter, dispersing litter everywhere in the general area of the litter tray. For this athletic style of litter user, there are several types of enclosed litter trays. These will help to keep the litter where it belongs.

Usually, when you purchase a cat or kitten from a Persian breeder, the breeder will provide you with an initial supply of the type of litter to which your cat has become accustomed. As a general rule it is wise to continue using the same kind of litter the breeder has provided. If you must make a change in litter, do so gradually by intermixing the familiar and the new brand or type of litter beginning with a greater proportion of the litter your cat prefers; continue this balance of old and new litter for a few weeks. Increase the amount of new-style litter gradually. You can eventually eliminate the old, familiar litter completely for your cat will quickly become accustomed to the brand you prefer. Cats prefer fixed routines. A change of litter when changing homes can cause problems in the new home and may upset the cat's security.

Place two to three inches of litter in the litter tray. When your cat uses the tray, remove soiled litter using a litter scoop. Dispose of used litter in a sanitary manner. Litter scoops are easily found in most pet supply shops. A durable, plastic scoop is preferable to plated metal. Either kind must, of course, be kept clean. For your sake and your cat's, keep the litter tray very clean. When you have visitors, nothing is more embarrassing than having one of them ask if you have a cat in the house because they have noticed an unpleasant odor. There is no reason for this to happen, for if you keep every item impeccably clean, the result will be an odor-free home.

It is also wise to place the entire litter tray on a washable rug or some newspaper which is four to six inches larger that the tray itself. There will always be a small amount of litter which ends up outside the litter tray. Cleaning time is made very easy, if you can roll up the papers or rug, when the tray is removed, taking any spilled litter away for proper disposal. Carefully roll up the papers or rug, taking any spilled litter away for proper disposal. The paper can be replaced with clean paper, or the rug can be laundered and replaced. Use bath mats as rugs. It is also helpful to know that some cats will make every effort to drag anything they find in the area surrounding the litter tray into the tray to serve as covering material. Your rug or papers may end up partially in the tray, so it's best to remove items near the litter tray.

If your Persian has trouble adjusting to a new litter tray, take some used litter from the old litter tray and place it in the new one. This will indicate that this shiny, new contraption is for your cat's own private use.

OTHER REQUIREMENTS

A few basic supplies that you will have to provide for your new Persian include a source of fresh, clean water, and food dishes. High-sided, ceramic crocks for both water and food are perfect because with these dishes Persians will not generally get that long ruff into the water or food while drinking or eating. Remember, if you begin with a kitten, you will need smaller versions of these important utensils than those required for your adult Persian.

It is important to establish a relationship with your cat's vet. If you do not know a vet, ask the breeder for suggestions. Always think of the vet as you would the family physician. If you always take your Persian to the same vet, a health history will be created which can be invaluable if your cat has a problem.

HOUSE RULES

So many people complain that they just are not able to keep their cat from jumping up on forbidden places such as a kitchen counter or a dining table. The cat is generally not the problem. From the very beginning when your Persian is introduced to your home, strict rules must be set as to where your new companion may and may not go. These rules must be followed with absolute rigidity. Cats can and do understand the idea of "never"; however, they are unable to comprehend the idea of "sometimes" or "on occasion". Your signals and actions must be consistent when dealing with your Persian companion.

Training your cat is similar to working with a very young child. With a child, at the early stages of socialization and language comprehension, you must repeat an idea or request many times before the child understands. Your cat is not as adaptable as a young child since people are able to generalize and animals are not able to do so. Therefore, you must work with your cat using a system based upon the idea that the "rules are the rules are the rules."

Once the house rules are established, your Persian will genially follow them unless some extraordinary circumstance occurs. Why does a well-adapted family companion suddenly lose all semblance of training and begin making "mistakes" on the bed or on some article of clothing? There generally are good reasons for this. The cat may be suffering with a physical problem which means seeking the assistance of your vet. Also, if someone in the house has broken one of the house rules, the cat may be reacting to mixed signals. Often, if the cat's mistakes are constantly on one family member's bed or personal items, this person may be the culprit who broke the rules. This can be something as simple as moving the cat's food dishes, failing to be consistent in feeding time, or failing to keep the cat's litter tray clean. If consistency and reliability are reintroduced to your Persian's routine, you will usually find that the problems soon disappear.

TRANSPORTING YOUR PERSIAN

Never take a cat anywhere without a suitable cat carrier. It is unwise to allow your cat the freedom to roam in your automobile your garden or back yard. In the car, a sudden loud noise can transform your cat into an unidentified flying object. Your cat might end up under your brake pedal or in your line of vision, a very dangerous situation when you are driving.

If you are transporting your Persian to the vet, you will find the experience a happier one if the cat is well-protected in a carrier. There are often other animals in the waiting room that can potentially upset your cat and whose contact might invite possible infection. Many vets require that your cat be in a strong, well-made carrier. If you have more than one cat, it is best to have a separate carrier for the use of each. This will create a sense of security since each cat will have christened the carrier with his or her own scent. Leave the open and well-lined carrier in a spot where the

A typical cat carrier. Never take your cat anywhere except in a suitable, well-protected carrier.

cat can use it as an alternative bed. This reinforces the feeling of security provided when you place your cat in his carrier for travel. Some cats will get into their carrier when you are about to leave the house for they love to be with you and to experience new sights and smells. Make sure that your Persian does not get caught inside the carrier as the lid or door can accidentally close. Always check a carrier which has been left out to make sure that the cat has not been trapped.

QUALITY TIME

One of the most satisfying experiences is the time spent maintaining your Persian's beauty. Since the Persian in a longhaired cat, *at least one quick combing is needed every day.* This is essential to ensure that the beautiful coat does not become a mass of snarls and tangles. Purchase a strong, metal comb which has wide teeth at one end and narrow teeth at the other. This will become one of your most useful tools in keeping your cat in top condition.

Every day you must carefully and quickly comb through your

This early cat Fancier, Mrs. Peter Brown, was photographed in the early 1900s. She patiently gives her prize cat a final touch-up before entering the ring.

Persian's coat. First use the wide-spaced teeth and then the narrow spaced teeth of the comb. This is a good time to check that your cat has not acquired any fleas. In warm climates, where fleas can abound humans can bring fleas into your home on their clothing. You will know there is a problem if you find small, black specks in your Persian's coat; these specks are flea droppings. There are good flea control powders, sprays, and shampoos available from your vet. You must also control fleas in the rugs, corners, and cracks in your home. This may sound difficult, but it is truly not a major problem with modern pest-control techniques. Just seek the advice of your family vet.

The sooner you begin the daily grooming ritual, the easier it will be for both you and your Persian. A kitten will want to play with the comb and will quickly tire of being held and combed. It is best to start slowly increasing the length of time and thoroughness of the combing over a period of weeks. You must establish that this activity is a necessary and important part of your routine.

Be cautious while combing in case there are any snarls or little mats in the coat which, if caught in the comb, will cause the hair to be

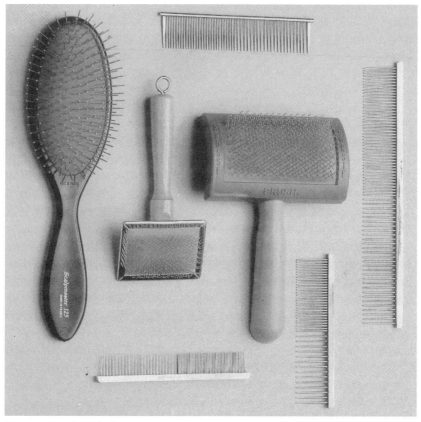

The essential tools for grooming.

pulled out with accompanying pain to your Persian. If you do discover a snarl, hold the snarled hair by the area closest to the cat's skin, and carefully work the comb through the top part of the mat (the portion farthest from the skin) removing it a bit at a time. By holding the base of the hair, you can avoid any hair pulling that would transmit pain to the cat. Working with an adult cat may take a little longer, and a more studied, gentle approach is necessary until you have established a mutual trust. Once established, you will learn that your Persian loves to be combed. Be cautious and do not pull hair out of the cat's coat; no animal appreciates having hair pulled. Occasionally you may find a knot or tangle which you cannot disentangle with the comb. Under exceptional circumstances, you may use scissors to make a few, careful snips. Never use pointed scissors. It is only safe to use round-tipped scissors and with great caution.

Your daily grooming session will remove the dead hair from your cat's coat and decrease the amount of hair your Persian might ingest during self-grooming.

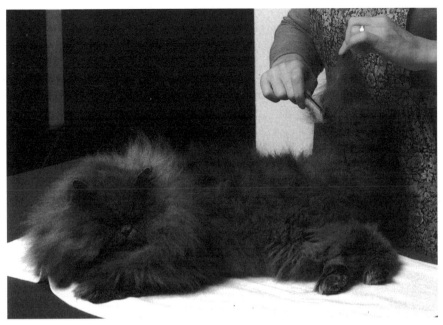

To keep the Persian in top condition, combing of the cat's tail and the rest of its coat should be a daily activity for the owner.

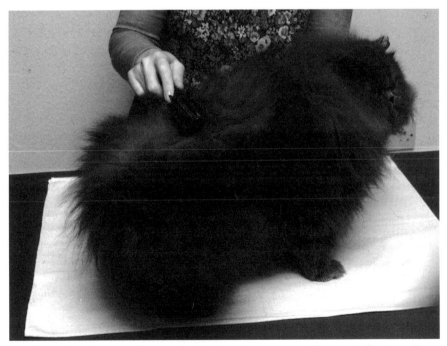

To obtain the best results, it is best to brush against a Persian's fur in order to achieve the effect of a sea of floating fur.

77

It is a good practice to comb the hair down on the Persian's stomach to remove any knots.

GENERAL MAINTENANCE

Carefully use a cotton swab to clean only the outer area you can see of your Persian's ears. There may be a small amount of ear wax. Never poke anything down your cat's ears. If there is any problem, check with your vet. The most common problem is ear mite infestation, which is easily detected, for the cat's ear will fill with dark, brown exudate. The cat will scratch and dig at the ear, and shake its head, since the ears itch when ear mite is present. This is a condition your cat's vet can treat and teach you how best to eliminate.

Be extremely careful in cleaning the ear's outer surfaces as the capillaries in the ear are very fragile. If you are over zealous and manage to rupture one, a bruise will appear.

You must carefully clip each of your cat's front and back claws occasionally. There are five on each front paw and four on each hind paw. You may find that your cat may not care to have the claws clipped, but it is essential to make this part of your maintenance program. If not clipped, the claws may curl under and enter the paw pad, creating a painful condition requiring surgical correction. Also, for showing a cat in the United States, it is a requirement that the claws be clipped.

BATHING YOUR PERSIAN

From time to time you will have to bathe your cat. Most cats do not really like water, except for drinking purposes. The only exceptions are the Turkish Van cats, who appear to find water irresistable.

Do not expect to find your Persian welcomes the bathing process. There will undoubtedly be struggles. Practice makes perfect and the time will eventually come when you will be able to tackle this procedure single-handedly. For the first few times it might be best to ask for assistance. Two sets of hands will be helpful to hold the wriggling, protesting cat, as will two sinks to do the bathing.

It is best to have the cat at convenient working height, in a sink, or on a table, rather than attempting to lean over your bathtub. The cat will feel more at ease and less threatened with this arrangement. As with grooming, it is wise to start the bathing process at a fairly young age — not later than four or five months. While your Persian may never really enjoy a bath, at least an attempt early in life may help your cat to realize that you are not trying to drown it.

Some shampoos are especially formulated for cats, but a suitable alternative, if you cannot find these, is to use a very mild, no-tears, baby shampoo. Double sinks are best—one for bathing and one for rinsing—but if you have only one sink—then stand a good-sized bowl on the draining board as a substitute for one of the sinks. A rubber pad in the sink or bowl will help keep your Persian from sliding around.

Be sure that you have every step carefully planned and have all necessary materials at hand before you begin, including, but not limited to:

- White (color-free) paper towels
- One or more large, soft towels which are only for your cat since cat hair will cling to them no matter how many times you launder them
- Your metal grooming comb
- A hair dryer
- A suitable cat or human baby shampoo
- Cotton swabs
- White vinegar

Cats are highly intelligent and perceptive animals. It is wise to make your plans and gather your equipment out of the cat's sight. If you do not, you may find that your Persian will realize what is pending and make a hurried exit.

With all materials gathered, you are ready to begin, and the sequence should be as follows:

1. Fill the sinks or bowls with warm water about four inches deep and test the temperature with your elbow, as you would for a human baby.
2. Give your Persian a careful combing to remove any knots and tangles you might find before you get the coat wet. Wetting a tangle or mat only makes it far worse.
3. Place small, easily-removable wads of slightly-dampened cotton wool in each ear to keep any water from running down into the ear canals. After the bath, remember to remove these.
4. Holding firmly, put your Persian into the water. There is absolutely no need for immersion and any attempt will terrify the cat. In all probability your Persian will tremble violently and shake as if freezing. Don't be alarmed. This is the average cat's reaction to water.
5. Wet the head first, being careful not to get water into your Persian's ears or eyes. Use a plastic beaker or jug and scoop the warm water over the cat's body, wetting it thoroughly. Some coats are difficult to wet to the skin because of their woolly texture. A wetting agent might be necessary.

One step before bathing a Persian is to comb the coat to remove any knots and tangles which will otherwise be made worse by wetting.

When bathing the Persian, rinse the coat with a hand-held shower. All traces of shampoo should be removed when rinsing or the coat will lose its "floating" appearance when dry.

6. Apply the shampoo, and work it up into a lather. A Persian's coat may be quite dense, so be thorough in this part of the procedure, including the tail and underparts. Keep the lather away from the cat's eyes. Use a soft cloth to gently wash the cat's face. Be very gentle, as the large eyes of a Persian can easily be scratched.

7. If possible, rinse the coat with a hand-held shower. If you do not have one of these, then rinse in several changes of water, pouring and scoop ing the water over your cat. By now you will see how very desirable it is that you get help from another pair of hands. It is essential that you remove all traces of shampoo from the coat or it will lose its beautiful, floating appearance when dry. Shampoo can leave an oily trace in the coat making it appear dull and heavy. A little white vinegar added in the final rinses will help to ensure that all shampoo is rinsed out. This is particularly important when your cat is in full and heavy coat.

8. Dry the fur by blotting with absorbent paper towelling or a cotton towel, but do not rub. Rubbing tends to tangle the coat. Then wrap your cat in a warm, dry towel and continue the blotting, gently pressing all over. Use of paper towelling is a great help in absorbing the water and helps to reduce the drying time. The best hair dryers to use are the large professional types used in some grooming shops, but as these are rather expensive, the average cat owner may not have one. Small hand-held hair dryers often emit a high-pitched sound which cats may find disturbing. Plugging the cat's ears with small pieces of dampened cottonwool will help a great deal in cutting back the intensity of the sound and the cat will probably relax, since the warm air from the dryer can be very soothing. Be careful to use the dryer on a warm set ting; you do not want to overheat your cat.

9. With the aid of a helper, gently play the warm air from the dryer over the cat's body, avoiding the eyes and ears. At the same time, comb and lift the fur as you direct the warm air toward it. This will prevent the curly or waved effect which results when the coat is not combed. Your aim is to keep all hairs separate and to accelerate the drying process. It is an important step in producing that beautiful, floating Persian coat.

10. Remove the damp cottonwool from the cat's ears.

11. Put your cat in a warm place for a few hours to ensure that the coat is absolutely dry. Breezes and cold air may cause illness, which can and should be avoided.

When bathing your Persian, remember that this is an exercise in mutual trust requiring gentle handling and studied care. Praise your cat a great deal during the bathing, drying, and grooming process. It will con-stantly reassure the animal. The result will please both you and your cat.

A Persian seems to know when it is beautiful.

Some breeders of white or Chinchilla Persians add a drop or two of bluing to the rinse water. Others may use a blue rinse for the final shampoo. This is applied to enhance the coat color. The rinse reflects light as it hits the coat, giving a purer, sparkling appearance. It is never permissible to modify or change a cat's coat color. To do so is cause for disqualification in the show ring. Some rinses may not be good for the health of your cat. Never forget that Persians lick their coats during self-grooming. If there is any question about the safety of a product, it is best not to use it.

Some differences are apparent between the grooming methods used in North America and in the rest of the world. First, there is the question of the use of talcum powder. American breeders of Persians prefer to use modern cat shampoos and conditioners, feeling there may be a possible health risk in the use of talcum powder. There are many excellent shampoos and conditioners available for cats, and at most shows there will be a pet stall selling them. However, the attitude is somewhat different in Great Britain and Europe where the vast majority of breeders and exhibitors still prefer the "old-fashioned" methods. None of them appear to have experienced any problems with the careful use of talcum powder and many of them feel that they can produce a more spectacular result in this way.

In applying talcum powder, breeders of white or lightly-colored cats often use baby talcum in the coat a few hours after the bath, when the fur is totally dry. It should be sprinkled in and combed through the coat, and will help to absorb any traces of oiliness in the cat's skin. It should be left in for two or three days, but must be totally removed before you show your cat. Failure to do so would result in disqualification. Again, a hand-held hair dryer and brush will easily remove all traces of talcum powder.

For richly-colored cats the normal baby talcum might tend to dull the gloss and shine of the coat. If the slightest trace is left it resembles dandruff. For these cats, some breeders use bran. Warm the bran in the oven first, then put it into a large tray. Stand the cat in the tray, and sprinkle, and gently rub the bran into the coat, leaving it for a while before removing it. Brush it out thoroughly in the same way as baby talcum.

The use of bran is essentially a British practice, which continues to work very successfully for a number of breeders in that country. In North America, however, the cat Fancy considers warm bran treatment an outmoded practice.

Finally, brush your cat with a pure bristle brush. By talking to other exhibitors and breeders at shows and elsewhere you will gain other useful tips. In general, you should brush always in the same sequence,

Talcum powder and brushes are standard grooming tools for some owners of Persians.

from the back to the front of the cat. Your aim is to make the coat stand up and away from the body, and for the ruff around the chest and neck to frame the head.

It should be noted that there are some breeders who are cautious about brushes feeling that by using them you risk pulling too much hair from the coat, particularly the tail. These people use instead a steel comb with wide teeth at one end and narrow teeth at the other. However, most breeders use brushes *and* combs for grooming, according to the particular task to be performed.

Many cat clubs and cat associations hold seminars and grooming demonstrations. Some of the advice you receive may flatly contradict that given here. Do not worry! As with most skills, there are a range of techniques. The advice we have given works well, but if you find other methods you prefer and which appear to work well for you and for your cat, do not hesitate to try them and make them part of the Persian's regular maintenance routine.

The Persian mother and her kittens will both require regular, daily grooming. Breeding Persians should not be contemplated unless the owner is prepared to take on these tasks.

CHAPTER V

REPRODUCTION

If you find the Persian cat glamorous and attractive and have a good specimen of the breed, then at some time you may consider plans to breed your Persian female. *Give very careful thought to the responsibilities incurred.* All too many kittens are produced each year that end up in the hands of the rescue societies or worse. No kittens should be produced

The horse-drawn cart of the Royal London Institution for Lost and Starving Cats, pictured around 1900. Founded in 1896, the Royal London Institution was one of the first cat rescue societies. Comparable organizations for homeless cats were founded around this time in Boston, Chicago, and Philadelphia.

without the commitment on the part of the breeder to assure that they will have lifelong, appropriate homes. *You should begin to plan the production of kittens only when you are quite sure that you will be able to find proper, caring homes for them all.*

Above all, dismiss from your mind any thought that you might make a substantial income from cat breeding. In our many years of experience in the cat world we have not met anyone who has made their fortune in this way. Bear in mind that the time and wide variety of expenses involved in the showing, breeding, and rearing of pet animals nearly always exceed any monetary return that you are likely to receive. If you feel that you really must breed kittens for the joy that this will bring to you and you are totally sure that you will find suitable homes for them, then forget any thought of monetary gain. Concentrate only on the delight and joy which a well-bred and well-mannered cat can bring.

The average litter of Persian kittens varies from two to five. Much pleasure can be gained from watching your Persian care for her kittens.

Do not be tempted into thinking that show success and fame in the cat world will follow quickly and easily. It will not. Of course you may be fortunate enough to have beginner's luck, and produce some superb show-quality kittens in your very first litter. It is more likely, however, that you will produce some fairly attractive ones that will be destined never to achieve much success on the show bench.

Be sure that your chosen female is from excellent stock, and that she conforms as nearly as possible to the Standard issued by one of the main cat registering bodies. *There is no point in perpetuating faults, genetic defects, or just poor-quality type (conformation).*

Do not forget that soon after the kittens are born you will need to begin gentle, regular grooming, as well as the daily grooming of your own Persian female, very time-consuming activities. *Do not even begin to attempt breeding Persians unless you enjoy grooming them.* If you regard grooming as just one of those time-consuming chores that cannot be avoided, then perhaps Persian cat breeding is not for you.

THE BREEDING QUEEN

Your young adult female is called a queen. Once she has reached adulthood, which usually occurs from about nine months onwards, she is

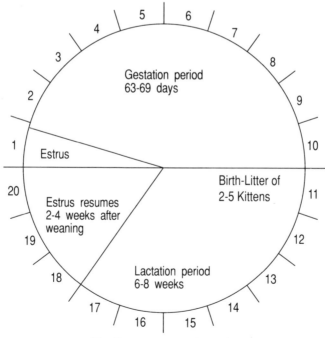

The Persian queen's cycle.

ready and probably eager to produce kittens during most of the year. In the world of responsible cat breeders, it is generally thought best to let her mature physically and psychologically before subjecting her to the drain of producing kittens. Most breeders of Persians cats prefer the females to be at least one year old before they have their first kittens.

Cats are seasonally polyestrus. Their seasons are associated with daylight length; once the shortest day of the year is passed and days begin to lengthen, the cat's system will rapidly prepare itself for reproduction. The peaks of her activity are likely to occur in the early spring and in late summer, although this is only a broad generalization. There are no hard and fast rules, and each female can be slightly different. In any case, although she may appear to be well grown physically, a female is not really mature enough for the birth and care of kittens until she is at least one year old. The demands of adequate nutrition for the growing kittens she is bearing will make it difficult for a very young queen. She might also have difficulties in the actual births because of the small size at that stage of her pelvic canal. In some Persians the first estrus period may not occur until she is eighteen months old. Siamese and other oriental breeds are much more precocious and often come into heat as early as five months.

A queen who has never been mated is known as a "maiden queen". She should not be mated at the time she shows the first signs of estrus. There is every possibility that she might conceive and produce kittens, but there is also a strong possibility that she will not. This "first call" will almost certainly occur before she is ten months old, and she is not yet ready for motherhood.

Although some breeders mate their queens more often, it is probably wiser not to let them have more than one litter a year so that their systems do not become weakened and depleted by frequent pregnancies, parturition, and the raising of their kittens.

ESTRUS

When your queen begins to mature physically, she will show the first signs of estrus. In this condition she is said to be calling or in heat or in season. Her reproductive organs have been undergoing various subtle changes in readiness for the stages of mating and fertilization, followed by pregnancy. As the days lengthen and daylight grows stronger, her brain sends signals to her hypothalamus to discharge gonadotropin releasing hormones (GnRH). This in turn stimulates the pituitary gland (at the base of her brain) to release two additional hormones.

One of these hormones is a follicle-stimulating hormone (FSH) which travels to her ovaries to generate growth of follicles in which her eggs will mature. The second hormone released from the pituitary gland is luteinizing hormone (LH). This is required to ensure development and maturation of her ovarian follicles. As the follicles develop, the ovaries will secrete estrogen, the hormone which is most responsible for the behavior of a female in season.

During this stage, known as preoestrus, she will become restless and will show you a great deal of extra affection. She will probably urinate more frequently, pace up and down, and if confined indoors, she will spend a good deal of time on window sills staring out of windows. If you leave doors ajar, even for a moment, she may make a dash for freedom. She is not yet ready to mate. Unlike a female dog, there will be no swelling of the vulva and usually no vaginal discharge.

After two to four days she will enter the second stage which is known as estrus, and during this period, she will allow mating to take place. The stage may be brief or may last up to about seven days or more. She will become increasingly agitated. Typical behavior is to roll on the floor and constantly rub her paws vigorously over her head. She will emit a characteristic howling cry known as calling. This sound can be quite disturbing. Novice cat owners have been known to rush their pet to the vet believing that their cat is desperately ill and in agony or great pain.

The queen is likely to lose interest in food and will almost certainly make quite determined efforts to escape from confinement in order to search for a mate. Her calling will probably attract a number of male cats which have not been neutered who will gather around in hopeful anticipation even if your cat is kept indoors. It is very important that you do not permit her any freedom during this period since there is no point in risking the eventual arrival of a litter of unwanted, non-pedigreed kittens.

If mating occurs during estrus, then the signs of estrus will diminish rapidly, usually within two or three days. On the other hand, if she is not mated, then the signs of estrus may continue for as long as eight to ten days. Then there will be a quiet period, known as diestrus, for a few weeks before the cycle begins all over again. Toward the autumn, as days become shorter and darker, most unbred queens will be out of season. They remain in a fallow state called anestrus until the reproductive cycle begins to stir once more as the days again begin to lengthen.

While your Persian queen is in estrus, her behavior may become rather anti-social. She may forget to use her toilet tray or may spray urine against soft furnishings, fabrics, and up against the walls in the house.

If you stroke her, she will adopt the mating position. Kneeling on her front legs with hindquarters raised resulting in a concave curvature (lordosis) to the spine, the tail swishing from side to side, and treading with her hind legs vigorously, she is likely to adopt this lordosis posture endlessly throughout the day accompanied by the vigorous tail swishing and howling.

NEUTERING THE PERSIAN QUEEN

If you do not plan to produce kittens from your female Persian at any time, you would be wise to have her neutered (spayed) by your vet. If she is allowed to continue coming into season without mating, she may develop ovarian cysts and might eventually develop cancerous growths or other complications which will endanger her health. The operation should not be done while she is in season since post-surgical bleeding is more difficult to control. Estrogen, present when a queen is in season, tends to prevent blood from clotting. Spaying is a routine operation with only minimal risks. Modern anesthetics and skilled veterinary techniques have made this a safe procedure.

SUPPRESSION OF ESTRUS

It is possible to seek help from your vet to suppress or postpone the onset of estrus. Some breeders have reservations about this, but it may sometimes become intolerable to live with a cat who is in an almost constant state of call. However vigilant you may be about open doors, at some time she may elude you and manage to escape to find a mate. The most widely-used drugs for this purpose are progestogens or progestins, such as megestrol acetate and medroxyprogesterone acetate, which are given either orally or by injection. After estrus-suppression using one of these drugs, it may be two or three months before your queen calls again after having received medication orally, or up to six months following an injection. Clearly, this is a course of action not to be undertaken lightly since residual amounts of these medications may be left in her system for some time.

Mating should not take place at a queen's first call following the use of such medication since conception may be prevented. Wait until the second call when her system should be clear of any residual trace amounts of the medication. Some breeders fear that kittens born after the use of progestogens may be harmed by this medication. There appears to be no evidence to support this fear. However, any prostagenic drug carries a risk of predisposing a cat to chronic endometritis (uterine infection), and the uterus is made more susceptible to opportunistic organisms under the influence of progesterone. Beware of continued usage of these powerful drugs.

PRELIMINARIES BEFORE MATING

A responsible owner will make sure that the queen is carefully checked over by a vet before taking her to a stud cat. Current practice is that all stud owners expect to be shown a certificate confirming that the queen is fully up-to-date with her inoculations and is in good health. Most stud owners will also require that a blood test be made within seventy-two hours of accepting the queen on their premises to show that she is completely free from Feline Leukemia Virus (FLV) and Feline Immunodeficiency Virus (FIV)—the cause of Feline AIDS. FIV belongs to the same family as the virus that causes AIDS in humans; however, it is important to know that there is no evidence that FIV can infect humans.

A sample of the queen's feces should be collected from her toilet tray and placed in a plastic bag or glass jar so your vet can check for any parasitic worms. The stool sample will be analyzed under a microscope, and, if necessary, medication will be prescribed. The vet will also check for external parasites such as ear mites or fleas.

You should also check for these on a regular basis. The presence of small black specks in the coat may indicate the presence of fleas. A dark brown or black, waxy discharge present in the ears will indicate the presence of ear mites. Control of fleas can easily be achieved with the use of a flea control product obtainable from your vet. Your vet can also supply you with medication to kill ear mites when necessary. None of these products should be used when kittens are due, or just after their arrival, as some of the products may be toxic to kittens under the age of twelve weeks. Clip your girl's claws. The owner of your cat's future mate will not thank you if your queen manages to rip a few pawsful of fur from her boy during the mating ritual.

CHOOSING THE STUD

Before your queen comes into estrus, you should make arrangements with the owner of a suitable stud cat. There are various ways of making this choice. It should be your aim to produce kittens of high quality; therefore, the correct choice of mate is important. Join any breed clubs which cater to your breed and color of cat. The club secretary will usually be able to give you helpful advice and will have lists of club members with male cats at public stud. Talk with the breeder of your Persian queen and discuss potential mates. The breeder should be well versed in the bloodlines with which you are working. Sound advice at this stage is very valuable and can help circumvent any potential problems. Keep in mind

Many beautiful and valuable trophies are offered.

Mrs. ROLLO WOODRUFF, Superintendent.

Send for particulars and prepare to enter your cats and attend the show.

A NEW BOOK ON THE CAT

We will have ready to mail in about two weeks a new book by Mrs. Barker, on

"How to Breed, Feed and Raise Cats and Kittens Successfully"

This book is a reprint of the series of articles that were run in the CAT JOURNAL last year. Printed on fine paper. Profusely illustrated. Paper Binding. Price, 25 cents. Address CAT JOURNAL.

Soiled Copies for about One-Third Price

We are sending large numbers of THE CAT JOURNAL to the News Stands. These are kept through the month on sale and all unsold copies are returned to us. Most of these are soiled and many of them slightly torn but nearly all clean on the inside pages. We will send you ten of these numbers all different, our selection for 40 cents in stamps. *Think of it* 160 pages of reading matter about cats and about 80 pictures or this small sum. Six numbers for 26 cents. Address THE CAT JOURNAL.

Ravenswood Hamish

Imported Orange—Registered U. S. R., N. C. C. R., C. C. R. "A distinct advance in type over anything seen yet." Our Cats II, 49. "The best Orange I have seen," Dick Whittington, December, 1901. Sire, Chubby ; grandsire, Champion Bundle. Winner First Championship Challenge Cup No. 14 and Special No. 17, Slough, 272 entries ; First Championship Challenge Cup No. 14, Special No. 192 and Medal No. 41, Brighton, 240 entries ; Second Manchester in same company a month later. Only times shown. Has always sired solid orange from mates of that color. At stud $15.00 to approved queens. Mrs. F. W. Story, 2368 N. Paulina Street, Chicago.

AT STUD

Arlington Hercules. Imported Sable Tabby. Grand head, massive frame. Lovely color and markings. 1st and specials Westminster, 1902. Fee, $15.00
Mrs. Sarmiento and Mrs. Cutler.

Arlington John Bull. Imported Pale Silver. Big boned, cobby cat, fine head and expression. Sires lovely kittens. Winner of many firsts and specials in England and America.
Fee, $15.00
Mrs. Sarmiento.

Shortly at stud, **Arlington Bur Abdul,** Imported Silver Tabby. Approved queens only. Terms cash at time of service.

Address, MRS. F. J. SARMIENTO
MRS. DWIGHT CUTLER
Arlington Place   -   -   -   Detroit, Mich.

LIGHT OF ASIA.

Pure White Persian, imported from Asia. Splendid Cobby type, perfect head, face short, large round orange eyes perfectly placed, small round ears, wide apart. Sires kittens

With Eyes of Deepest Blue.

SWAMSCOTT

Swamscott

Pure white blue eyed strain. Immense coat of the finest quality, great style, gentle disposition.

MOON EYES.

Brown Tabby, small white points. Bred by Mrs. E. N. Barker, son of the celebrated King Humbert.

Fee for Either $10.

MRS. FRED EVERETT SMITH,
1849 Melrose St., Chicago, Ills.

KING OF THE SILVERS
Imported.

Sire Bitterne, Silver Chieftain, grandsire Champion Lord Southhampton. Very large, splendid head and coat. Winner of 2 firsts, specials and reserves at London shows. OLD FORT CATTERY

JACK FROST, the palest silver stud this side of the water. On account of his youth he will serve only a limited number of queens. Fee $25
OLD FORT CATTERY, AKIN, N. Y.

"Paris" No. 188 B. C. C. S. B.
AT STUD

King of Brushwood

Pure white strain, with blue eyes. Winner of Gold Medal, 1898, Milwaukee ; 1st and three specials, Chicago, 1901 ; Silver loving cup for Best Male in Beresford Cat Club ; medal for Best White Cat Male or Female ; $5 in Gold for Best Male in Show. Sire of seven prize-winners, among them four firsts, Chicago, 1901. Fee $10. Address,
BRUSHWOOD CATTERY,
7306 Bond Avenue, Chicago.

Black Cupid
Splendid solid black — yellow eyes—good head ,black to his skin—heavy coat.

First and two specials at Cincinnati, 1902.   Fee, $10.
MRS. J. S. OWEN,
OWENA CATTERY,
282 Hudson Ave., DETROIT, MICH.

COMET AT STUD. Fee $10
(White Queens Only)

Prize Winner B. C. C. Show 1901 and 1902

Pure White Persian with Deep Blue Eyes and Sound Hearing

ELITE CATTERY, 264 Leavitt Street, Chicago

Champion His Majesty

Thoroughbred white Persian, son of Royal Norton Magnificent head and shape. Perfect disposition. Sires wonderfully coated cobby kittens. Winner of many firsts and specials. For information, etc., address Rosedale Kennels, Melrose, Mass.

PROSPER LE GAI
Blue-eyed, white.

DONALD
Solid orange.

Each first in their class at Cleveland, 1902. Fee for either $10. Wayne Cattery, Wayne, Mich.

Rookwood Emperor III. Gray Tabby, registered. Won first and several specials at Cincinnati, Ohio. Perfect shape, short face, orange eyes. Fee $5. Rookwood Cattery, Newport, Ky.

Blue Eyed. White, very fine. Fee $10.
Black Persian. Stud fee $10. Mrs. C. L. Wagner, Sandusky, Ohio.

Onyx (known in England as Melton Pearl). Imported silver tabby ; sired by Windsor Beetle, grandson of Lord Southhampton. Sires beautiful kittens with immense coats. Fee $10. Cherycroft Cattery, Mrs. Alma J. Wright, Phelps, N. Y.

White Huzzar. Imported, white, deep blue eyes ; won 2d as kitten, England, 1900; 1st and special N.Y. 1902. Limited number of Queens booked now for season ending April 1st. Fee, $15.00. Mrs. Brian Brown, 504 Pacific St., Brooklyn, N. Y.

King C., S. B. A., No. 180, Fine Black Persian. Fee $10. G. R. Cairnes, Mansfield, Ohio.

PEDIGREE BLANKS.

Keep a pedigree record of your kittens. It is much easier done if you have a blank that is printed especially for this purpose. We furnish them at 15 cts. per dozen or 25 for 25 cts. Order from the CAT JOURNAL office.

A page from a 1903 issue of *The Cat Journal,* published in Palmyra, New York, advertized top quality Persian studs in the early days of the cat Fancy.

that *the purpose of any breeding is to improve the breed.*

Your cat's breeder will have a very detailed knowledge of appropriate studs for your queen's bloodlines. Attend as many cat shows as possible and take every opportunity to talk to other breeders. Most well-established breeders are delighted to be helpful to novices. At these shows you will be able to see many of the male cats. Study pedigrees and determine which combinations or bloodlines tend to produce the highest proportion of winning kittens and cats. It is likely that the ideal mating for your queen will be a stud cat with similar bloodlines to hers or from a family or line that has crossed well with the female's bloodline in the past.

However, to a certain extent , there is a good deal of trial and error in finding a prize-winning combination. This is one of the features that makes the breeding of pedigreed animals such an exciting challenge. Undoubtedly you should look into the possibility of using the *sire* of a currently fashionable and prize-winning Persian. After all, it was that prize-winner's father who helped produce the younger prize-winner. In choosing a stud for your queen, you should look to his bloodline to supplement or provide those qualities which may perhaps be lacking in your own cat. Because of the complexity of genetics, it is almost certain that your potential success will be based not only on knowledge but also upon a large portion of good luck.

STUD-SERVICE CONTRACTS

It is not unreasonable to expect the stud cat's owner to give you a stud-service contract. This contract does not need to be long, complicated, and full of legal jargon. Both parties should sign and keep a copy of the agreement. The contract should clearly state the stud fee, the length of time for which the stud owner is prepared to care for your cat, and whether or not the stud cat's owner will be prepared to give a free mating at a later date if your queen fails to conceive or loses her kittens for any reason. Also, any other contingencies which either party may wish to cover should be carefully spelled out. It is wise to avoid "pick of the litter" arrangements in lieu of your paying a stud fee. These arrangements are fraught with hazard, complications, and all too often lead to bitter enmities—or worse.

PRELIMINARIES TO BREEDING

It is usual to transport your queen to the stud owner's home in a secure basket or cat carrier on the second or third day of estrus. Your queen will establish a pattern of the number of days during which she is in heat. This is another reason to wait until a female is at least a year old. Some cats may be in heat a mere two or three days, others for several days. Depending upon your cat's heat cycle, you will be able to determine which would be the best day for taking her to the male. It is also common for the female to establish a regular length of time for estrus, such as being in heat for six days, then out of heat for twenty days, followed by being in heat for six days, etc. The occasions when each female's cycle repeats can be determined through careful observation. Don't depend on your memory to keep track of these cycles. Mark them on a calendar so that you will have no question when you wish to take her to be bred. When the perfect moment arrives, take your queen to the stud owner's premises for the mating. Because the stud is happier and more at ease in his own surroundings, he is never transported to the queen's premises where he may refuse to perform. In any case, the female's owner probably will not have the proper accommodation for him.

In a male cat's own stud quarters, he will already have increased his feelings of safety and security by rubbing against the surroundings leaving the smell from his scent glands, and further delineating his territory by spraying. It is this perfectly normal behavior which usually makes it impossible to keep an entire or non-neutered male indoors. His natural territorial scent-marking results in a very pungent smell which persists, and which most humans find intolerable.

NEUTERING THE MALE PERSIAN

If you have no plans to become involved in breeding, a sensible decision when purchasing your first Persian is to choose a male. The male in the animal world is usually more coated and impressive looking than is the female and a male Persian will soon grow into a splendid and magnificent young animal. However, there is no way you can live with an entire, unneutered male cat indoors. At around the age of six months you should take advice from your vet and have the cat neutered. Left entire any later, a male Persian will probably start to spray.

The neutering operation is simple and quick. Your vet will almost certainly ask you to leave your cat in the morning, and will then telephone you later in the day to say that your cat is ready for collection. The cat may look a trifle sorry for himself, and still a little groggy from the anesthetic, but by the following morning will be behaving as though nothing has happened. A return trip to the vet about seven days later for stitches to be removed, and the entire procedure is complete.

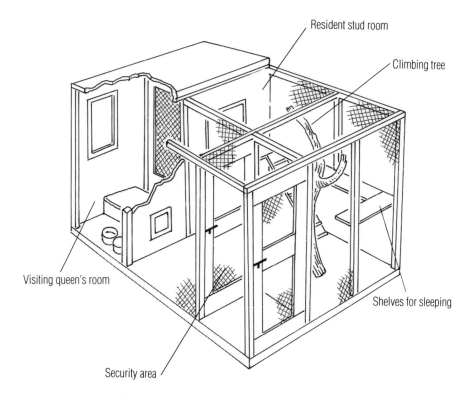

Resident stud room

Climbing tree

Visiting queen's room

Shelves for sleeping

Security area

The ideal stud house provides multi-compartments with exclusive accomodation for the stud and a comfortable, secure pen for the visiting queen.

THE COURTING PERIOD

The settling-in period for your queen may be fairly brief, or it may take two or three days. The stud cat's owner often leaves the queen in a suitable basket or other container in the stud's quarters, where the male may sniff around and investigate, so that they both become used to each other without any actual physical contact. A young, inexperienced queen may show every sign of shyness — even though she is calling. Alternatively, faced with a sex-starved male, even the gentlest female may react quite viciously.

When the stud owner feels that a bond, or at least a mutual interest, has been established, the two cats can be allowed to make physical contact. The stud's owner will usually keep quietly out of the way nearby, but be prepared with a blanket and perhaps a wide broom in case a quick separation of the two is required. Occasionally, a male cat may attack the female quite ferociously. This is not common, but, if it happens, you may well have to start your search for the ideal mate all over again since it is likely in these circumstances, that these two particular cats will never mate.

SUCCESSFUL MATING

Very little human cooperation is needed for cats to mate successfully. In fact, any attempt to help may result in your receiving some very nasty bites or scratches. It is certainly a case of letting nature take its course. In most cases, after the queen has been put in the stud's quarters, she will settle down happily and begin to make burbling or singing noises to encourage and entice the male. When the stud owner decides that the mutual interest is sufficient to allow them to meet, it is time to release the female from the basket or carrier very cautiously. A mating mat for the cat's use should be supplied by the owner of the male. A washable piece of carpet is ideal for this purpose so that the pair may get a good grip on the mat without slipping and sliding around.

The queen will adopt the mating posture: down on her front legs with her hindquarters raised, her tail to one side, and paddling or treading with her back legs. The male will cautiously approach her, and, after some initial investigation and sniffing, he will shift to her side and rear before pouncing and holding her down with his teeth firmly, but carefully, clamped on the loose skin on the back of her neck. He will straddle her, maneuvering quickly for entry. If she is not in the most convenient mating position, the experienced stud may use his back legs to coax her into a lower or more accessible position. At the appropriate moment, he will arch his back and begin thrusting motions. With her tail flicked over to one side, he will lower himself and enter her. Ejaculation and separation are completed in about ten seconds.

When she is entered, she will often give a piercing shriek or high-pitched scream, and you may well be horrified and think that she is being seriously damaged. The scream is normal and nothing to worry about. The sound, which may well include low-pitched, almost growling sounds from the female, is the sound of procreation in the feline world—an announcement to the world that new lives are about to begin. The natural course of feline procreation includes these primitive howls and yells of mating.

Most stud owners will have provided a high shelf or a chair in the stud's quarters so that the male may beat a hasty retreat to a place of safety upon completion of the mating ritual. It sometimes happens that the gentle, sweet, and endearingly affectionate queen will decide she wants an all-out, no-holds-barred fight with her mate. She will almost certainly lash out at him with her claws unsheathed, as he leaps clear after having completed the mating. The queen will calm down in a few minutes and let her mate approach again. In the meantime, she will roll vigorously on the ground. After this, they will both settle down to washing and cleaning. Soon after, unless they are separated, the lovers will be ready for a repeat performance. It is quite usual to allow the cats three or four matings over a period of two days.

Sometimes one mating is all that is required to induce ovulation; however, most stud owners prefer to allow several matings to increase the certainty of ovulation and impregnation. Unlike most other mammals, the female cat does not release eggs from her ovaries until after mating has taken place. Female cats do not ovulate until copulatory stimulation has occurred. In this behavior, they are similar to the mink, rabbit, or ferret. Ovulation occurs about twenty-four to thirty-six hours after mating and ensures that there are viable sperm cells present to fertilize the eggs.

Keep in mind that even though your female has been mated (and probably three to four times), she can still be bred by other males if she is allowed contact with them while she remains in heat. It is not uncommon for a female to produce kittens which have been sired by several different males when she is allowed to roam about the neighborhood during her heat cycle. Therefore, keep your female well-protected until she is completely and unquestionably out of heat. Once pregnant and no longer in heat, she will remain out of heat until her kittens have been delivered and are well on their way to a state of independence.

FERTILIZATION

When your queen has been mated, a signal is sent from the nerve endings in the cervix via the nervous system to the brain. The signal is received by the hypothalamus which emits GnRH followed by a subsequent release of LH from the pituitary. When these hormones reach the ovaries in sufficient strength, the follicles rupture, and release their eggs. This complex process takes place most generally around twenty-four to thirty-six hours after mating but may occur up to fifty hours afterwards. Once released, the eggs make their way into the fallopian tubes, there to be fertilized by the waiting sperm.

Back home, your queen will soon settle down and behave in her normal fashion. It is important that you vary her diet with any nutritional supplement your vet deems necessary.

GESTATION

The period of time from mating to the birth of kittens averages sixty-five days. It may be two, three, or even four days less, or even a few more; but experienced breeders expect the kittens to arrive on or around the sixty-fifth day. Keeping in mind that eggs are not released until after mating, queens producing their kittens slightly later than you may have calculated, may in fact be producing them in the normal number of days from the actual time of fertilization. Our experience has been that each queen establishes her own definite pattern which her system generally follows with respect to the amount of time from impregnation until her kittens are born. If your Persian takes, for example, sixty-six days before giving birth, chances are that she will always take sixty-six days unless there are some unforeseen complications which would require veterinary assistance. This makes it convenient for you to be able to plan the arrival of kittens on a day when you will definitely be present—something some queens insist upon when they are giving birth.

PREGNANCY

If fertilization has taken place, the first signs of pregnancy will be when the queen's nipples begin to swell and take on a rosy-colored appearance. Known as pinking-up, this is particularly noticeable in the young, first-time queen. At about this time she will begin to radiate happiness and contentment and should appear glowingly healthy. At this stage her babies are less than half an inch long, and yet they will already contain a form of respiratory system, limbs, skull, tail, and a urogenital system. Continue with her normal diet, but do not overfeed her so that she becomes too fat. Excess weight may well complicate parturition.

The period when most congenital malformations occur is from the twelfth to the eighteenth days of pregnancy. There is little that can be done to prevent malformations, but there are certainly a few mistakes which should be avoided by the queen's owner. Do not attempt to breed a Persian showing any signs of ringworm. The accepted treatment for this condition is a month's course of Griseofulvin, more popularly known a Fulvicin, an anti-fungal medication in tablet form which is given orally every day. *This drug is potentially harmful to developing embryos as are some of the modified-live panleukopenia vaccines.* An excess of vitamin A at this stage, or of steroids, may cause problems. Indeed, a wide range of medications are potentially harmful. It is imperative that you consult your vet for any potential nutrition or medication problems. Above all, don't try to be a home style, self-educated cat doctor.

Around the fourth week of pregnancy it is possible for a vet to feel the tiny embryo kittens by careful palpation. This is not the sort of examination which an amateur should attempt since it is all too easy to induce an abortion or cause damage to the embryos or to the queen. At this stage, it would make sense to use modern techniques and ask your vet to check the number of growing embryos by doing an ultrasound scan. This is a comparatively inexpensive procedure with absolutely no risk to the queen or to the embryos. At this stage, some breeders like to add a small supplement of bone meal in the ratio of one dessert-spoonful to a pound of meat. Other breeders assume that since they take vitamin supplements themselves, then the same additives might be good for their pets. Veterinary opinions say that if the diet is good, there is no need at all for vitamin supplements.

When the fifth week of pregnancy has been reached, the queen's abdomen will be swollen and her nipples quite prominent. She will need extra food. Now is the time to supplement her diet by the introduction of a mid-day meal consisting of high-quality protein food. Do not increase the size of her breakfast or evening meals. It is unkind to overload her already plump abdomen with too much food. Your aim is to get good, healthy, muscular tone—not a fat, overfed cat.

During the sixth week, it is a good idea to boost your queen's calcium reserves which are being depleted because of the development of her growing kittens. This can be accomplished by giving her diluted, evaporated milk to drink. Cows' milk is a good source of calcium; but, unless your pet has been drinking it regularly since her kitten days, her system may not easily assimilate it. As a result, she may suffer from diarrhea which is certainly one of the last things you want with a Persian queen at this stage of her pregnancy. Some breeders use calcium supplements bought from their pet shops. However, in our experience, a balanced diet is best during pregnancy. Too much calcium supplement can cause an imbalance before and around parturition; i.e., her system has lots of calcium but cannot utilize it.

Check her bowel movements. If they become too hard, they could cause some obstruction to the pelvic canal. If her feces is hard, give her a teaspoonful of liquid paraffin or olive oil. This can be administered most easily by using a syringe or large eye dropper inserted into the side of her mouth. Even so, be prepared for her to reject the oil by vigorously shaking her head or spitting it out. As a precaution, remember to cover your clothing.

During this exciting period there is not a great deal the owner can do to help other than to provide a continued, good, nourishing diet, and to see that the pet gets enough exercise. Unlike oriental cats, Persians do not generally take to the idea of exercise with any enthusiasm. More often than not, they like a gentle, plodding, and frankly, rather lazy, sybaritic existence. So, encourage her to chase small fluffy toys or pounce after a trailed piece of string. We also find that queens love a gentle tummy rub as they get larger and larger. This gentle massage will produce a feeling of trust and companionship which may help your queen during delivery. If you are there, all will be well as far as she is concerned.

During this last month of pregnancy the queen's total food intake should be gradually increased until she is receiving between a third and a half more food than usual—depending on her appetite. Around this time you should begin to cut down the carbohydrates and increase the protein. Extra vitamin A should be given during this last stage of pregnancy. Cod liver oil is a good source and she will probably love it.

KITTENING

During the seventh and eighth weeks the queen will probably begin to search for suitable nesting places where she may quietly have her kittens. Her own ideas are seldom suitable as she is likely to decide that the airing cupboard, a corner of your favorite closet which contains your very best clothes, or somewhere quite inaccessible to all humans, perhaps even under your bed in the farthest corner, are the perfect places.

The ideal spot is probably your own bedroom where curtains can be drawn to keep out bright sunlight. There you will be on hand if help is needed during the night either during the births, or for the week or so after kittening. Our experience has shown that quite often, queens will wait until we are present to begin delivery.

A kittening box is essential. Many shops sell somewhat complicated and expensive ones. It is difficult to do better than to use easily disposable items such as a large, rigid cardboard box, about two feet or so wide, slightly longer in length, and about two feet in height. The box should be wiped out with a mild disinfectant. Avoid disinfectants containing phenols or coal tar products, which are dangerous to cats. Line the bottom of the box with several layers of clean newspaper and cover these with layers of paper towels or clean, cotton cloths, all of which may be disposed of when soiled. The box should be large enough for your expectant mother to stretch out, but small enough for her to press against the sides with her feet when she is in labor. A removable lid which will allow easy access should be found. Cut a round hole, about seven to eight inches in diameter, about five or six inches above the floor, in one side of the box, similar to a cat flap so that she can come and go as she pleases. In this box she will feel safe and secure, and you can gain easy access via the removable lid.

If the room is too cold, pet shops sell small, electric heating pads, about 10" x 12" in size for use in the bottom of kittening boxes. These can provide comfort to the queen and will encourage her to use the box before the kittens are due. Be careful that the pad temperature is not set at too high a temperature. The pad should be placed under some of the towel layers at the bottom of the box. Be sure that a litter tray is nearby in case she needs it and, of course, keep it scrupulously clean at all times. Maintain a bowl of fresh, clean water nearby, but away from the litter tray.

Check her nipples regularly. At any sign of dryness gently massage them with pure vegetable oil or olive oil. It is a good idea to cut away the surrounding hair with blunt-nosed scissors, and also trim away the coat immediately surrounding her genital area. This hair will soon grow back and the shortening will help her to clean herself more easily. Many breeders also trim back the fur on the entire belly area. This will make it much easier for the young kittens to gain access to her nipples and will help to prevent any caking-over caused by dried milk.

You should wash the nipple area gently with water-softened cotton wool or a very soft, clean cloth. If you find any slight crusting on the nipples themselves, moisten them thoroughly with warm olive oil, and the crusting should easily come off. Experienced breeders like to check the temperature of their pregnant queens around the sixtieth day of her pregnancy and onwards. A thermometer slightly covered with petroleum jelly, should be gently introduced a very short way into her rectum. Standard temperature at this time should be around 101.5° F (38.5° C). A sudden drop to 98°F (36.5°C) or 99° F (37° C) will herald the arrival of kittens within the next twelve hours. If her temperature rises by two or three degrees, call your vet without delay. It is wise to familiarize your pet with the temperature-taking technique well beforehand to avoid terrifying her during this critical time.

If kittens are born before the sixtieth day they will be immature and have considerably less chance of surviving. Do not panic if the queen passes her due date by a day or two. Up to sixty-eight days is not completely unusual, providing she has shown no signs of pushing or straining and her temperature is normal. If nothing has happened by the sixty-eighth day, ask your vet to check that all is well.

Slight vaginal bleeding is not a cause for alarm. However, be on the lookout for any unusual signs such as mild-to-heavy bleeding or any other discharge. It is wise under these circumstances to call your family vet rather than risk any complications which might ensue. He will check for fetal heartbeats, or the absence of them, and make a decision as to the possible need for a Cesarean delivery, or some other course of action.

You should have no problems over ambient warmth for spring or summer kittens. At other times of the year it would be wise to ensure that the room in which the births are to take place is maintained at an even, warm temperature. *A common cause of kitten mortality is hypothermia.* For kittening, it is best to keep the room temperature minimally at 72° F (22° C). This may not be entirely comfortable for you, but must be endured for a week or so, until the kittens have become well established.

FELINE MIDWIFERY

Shortly before delivery, the queen will have a small vaginal discharge. This will be followed by loud purring, faster breathing, and is often accompanied by rapid kneading motions with her front paws. If she is a young maiden queen, she will probably be restless and will want to pace up and down. A more experienced queen is likely to rest quietly in her kittening box spending time happily shredding the paper lining for her nest. Persian queens generally become very attached to their owners and will almost certainly want the comfort of your presence. Some queens will actually hold back until their owner is present for the birth, although a few will prefer to get on with it without any help or company.

Cats usually lie on their sides while giving birth, but do not be alarmed if your queen prefers to stand and deliver. Uterine contractions will begin as the first kitten slowly moves down into the cervix from the uterus. The contractions will gradually increase in frequency peaking at up to one every thirty seconds. This stage may last for some hours. The novice should call the vet if the first kitten is not born within one or two hours after the onset of the cat's straining. Just before the birth of the first kitten, if everything is going normally, a dark, greyish sac of fluid may be passed. This is quite normal, and you should note the time carefully to ensure that the first kitten follows within the next hour, but no more than two.

Each kitten will usually be enclosed in a placental membrane known as the amniotic sac and be surrounded by a straw-colored liquid. Sometimes the sac is ruptured in the birth process, and when this occurs the liquid is discharged from the queen's vulva. The newspapers in your kittening box will absorb any fluid, and can be disposed of later. When the contractions are coming at regular intervals, you will see the amniotic sac appear at the vaginal opening. Ideally each kitten should be born in the sac. Occasionally, a kitten will partially appear, and then seem to get stuck half-way out. A little assistance may be needed. Use a piece of clean terry toweling and gently pull downwards during a contraction. Never pull upwards or sideways.

Immediately after birth, the kitten will stretch its neck and the mother will remove the sac from the kitten using her rough tongue. If she fails to do this, then quickly do it for her so that the kitten can breathe. If you fail to do this, you may lose the kitten. Use a small piece of terry toweling to rub gently on the top of the kitten's head. This will loosen the sac so that it can easily be peeled off. The queen should continue to lick and clean the kitten to stimulate its breathing. If she does not do so, you must make sure the kitten's air passages are clear by wiping away any fluid from its face. Brisk rubbing with toweling should stimulate breathing. If this fails, try blowing very gently into its nostrils; then rub briskly with toweling with the kitten's head held downwards and carefully supported by your fingers. The baby will probably complain loudly. This means you are getting some air into its lungs.

The umbilical cord should be severed by the queen. The placenta or afterbirth which was attached to the wall of the uterus, will be expelled after the kitten, and the queen will sever the cord by eating the placenta and cord, up to a point about three-quarters of an inch to one inch from the body of the kitten.

Novice breeders may find the eating of the placenta a slightly disturbing occurrence, but it is very necessary and quite natural. It supplies the new mother with the various nutrients and hormonal substances that her system needs. The placenta resembles a small piece of liver. Count the number of placentas carefully. One should be accounted for after the birth of each kitten. The new mother does not need to eat them all. If there is any doubt that a placenta may have been retained, contact your vet, who will give the queen a shot of oxytocin to expel any remaining pla-

The newborn Persian kitten should be protected from strong light.

cental pieces. Anything left internally may give rise later to infections.

If your queen fails to bite through the umbilical cord, then you may need to sever it yourself. Some breeders recommend the use of blunt scissors, clamps, and white iodine. In fact, it is perhaps ideally done by very carefully breaking the cord gently about an inch or so from the kitten's body with your own spotlessly-clean fingers. The ends of the cord will seal simultaneously. Be careful not to pull on the cord or you may cause an umbilical hernia in the kitten.

Some breeders think it is a good idea to remove newborn kittens briefly to a warm, lined box near to the mother while she is giving birth to the next kitten. They should be returned to her quickly after each birth is complete. The newborn kittens only need to be removed from the box if the queen is thrusting and moving from side-to-side, with the possibility of rolling over, inadvertently, on one of her fragile babies.

THE NEW MOTHER

The average litter of Persian kittens varies from two to five, and only rarely are there more than five. Six or seven is most unusual although not unknown. After the last kitten has arrived, the kittening box should be cleaned up and all soiled material carefully disposed. Soft cloths can now be placed over the newspaper for bedding. Cotton is best. Avoid loosely woven material in which the baby kittens may get their tiny, but sharp, claws caught. After all the kittens have been born, the mother will settle down happily to nurse and suckle her babies. She will probably appreciate some warm, diluted, evaporated milk with a teaspoonful of glucose added. The new mother will not leave her babies for the first few hours, so food and drink will have to be taken to her. Make sure that all the kittens are suckling, and, if necessary, guide them to an appropriate nipple. Place them just under the nipple, as they always tend to reach upwards.

You should be able to relax and enjoy the delight and joy of watching your Persian queen care for her babies. Maintain a low light level until the newborns' eyes have been open for several days. The mother will know when it is time for her kits to leave the nest. Each time you quietly look into the nesting box, be sure to praise your mother cat and tell her how much you appreciate her being such a good mother to her kittens. This reassurance will help keep her calm and secure. Otherwise, she may well begin the practice of hiding kittens. There is nothing more stressful to the human companion than having to search for the newborn litter when the mother cat believes that your arrangements lack some essential feature. The key is to keep her warm, calm, secure, well-praised, and in semi-darkened surroundings. There can be few sights more beautiful than that

A day old kitten, its eyes remain closed for the first six to twelve days of life.

of a contented mother washing her kittens to the accompaniment of ecstatic purrs.

POSTPARTUM

Always expect a certain small amount of bleeding following kittening. However, if this becomes excessive, the queen will become weak. This could be a sign of serious problems, and your vet should be contacted without delay. Sometimes, fortunately rarely, an inflammation of the womb, known as metritis, may develop after kittening. You will see and smell an unpleasant discharge which will be darkish brown in color. Call your vet immediately, or you will lose both the queen and the kittens. A careful course of antibiotics will most likely be needed.

Mastitis, an inflammation of one or more of the mammary glands, can occur a week or two after kittening. The affected gland appears red and swollen and it will probably feel unusually warm. Again, consult your vet since a course of antibiotics will be needed.

In some cases, a lack of sufficient calcium in the new mother's system will produce spasms and fits, a condition called eclampsia. Even if you have been supplementing her diet with additional calcium, the queen may not have properly absorbed it. This condition must be given immediate attention by your family vet. Surprisingly, a simple calcium injection will alleviate this condition almost immediately.

REARING YOUR KITTENS

Kittens are born with their eyes closed. When the eyes open eventually between six to twelve days after their birth, you will discover that the eye color is blue. Do not be dismayed. They will change to the correct color as the kittens grow. During this closed-eye period, any strong light will be distressing to the kittens, so, keep the room moderately dark or shaded. Do not expose them to full light until after their eyes are fully opened. They will spend their first few weeks suckling from their mother.

At around four weeks of age, they will become very adventurous and will start running around and exploring. At this time they will be growing their first teeth. you should now begin to get them interested in solid food. As with humans, a well-balanced and varied diet is best. Experienced breeders have their own favorite diets which usually consist of finely shredded and chopped rabbit or chicken; carefully de-boned, cooked fish; finely minced liver (only very small quantities); diluted, tinned milk; and chopped, hard-boiled egg. A number of well-balanced and excellent brands of kitten food are available from pet stores. Once you have the kittens interested in solid food, make sure that a shallow litter tray is available. Their mother will teach them how to use it.

Food should be put on flat plates for kittens. Remember that their

Kittens should suckle their mother for about four weeks after birth and then should be weaned on to solid foods.

stomachs are extremely tiny; only small amounts of food will be needed. They should be fed frequently throughout the day at about three-hour intervals so as to allow for proper digestion between feedings. When they are about three to four months of age, the meals may be cut back to three or four times a day. At the age of five or six months, two meals each day are adequate. Always have fresh, clean water available. Change the water at least twice a day—even if the kittens do not appear to be drinking from it.

At about six weeks of age the mother will begin to leave the kittens to their own resources. At eight weeks, they should be removed from their mother during the daytime (if they are adjusting well to eating solid food) and returned to her at night. Innoculations should be given when the kittens are about ten weeks old. Take your vet's advice on this very important matter. The kittens you have decided to sell should go to their new homes at about twelve weeks of age.

Persian kittens aged sixteen weeks. They have reached the age when they can leave their mother and go to new homes.

Cat shows today can be large affairs, such as the Supreme Cat Show, held every December at the National Exhibition Centre in Birmingham, England.

CHAPTER VI:

SHOWING AND JUDGING

There are two basic types of cat show. The first style of show is open to the general public from beginning to end, with the owners of the exhibits present during the entire judging process. This style of show is prevalent throughout the United States and Europe with the exception of Great Britain.

Early cat shows like the Richmond Show of 1903 pictured here, were often held out-of-doors under tents.

The owners or stewards at these shows take the exhibits from their cages to a judging area for evaluation. At the completion of the judging process, the cats are then returned to their benching cages to await the exciting moment when the top exhibits are asked to return to the judging area for the finals, where the awards, including best in show, are announced.

Spectators can learn valuable information at shows, like this one in the United States, where the judges point out the outstanding points of the winning cats.

Final awards are generally accompanied by the officiating judge's discussion of the fine points of each of the winners. It is during discussion that spectators and Persian owners can learn the most regarding exactly how a top example of the breed and color being discussed appears to the trained eye. Each of the outstanding features of the winners is explained by the judge so that everyone can gain a better appreciation of the ways in which that particular exhibit meets its standard of perfection. A rosette is awarded, indicating the particular award the cat has won. Sometimes a trophy is also awarded along with the rosette.

It is important to keep in mind that the judge compares each exhibit to its Standard to determine which exhibit, in that judge's opinion, most closely fits that Standard. All exhibits are evaluated against their Standard as opposed to being evaluated against each other.

CAT SHOWS IN THE BRITISH COMMONWEALTH

The other general style of show, which is quite popular throughout the countries in the British Commonwealth, is open to the general public and the owners of the exhibits, only *after* the completion of the Open class judging. These shows are usually open for visitors in the early afternoon.

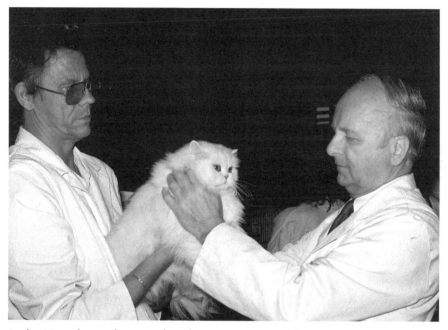

In the United Kingdom, each judge, accompanied by a steward, moves from cage to cage to evaluate each exhibit.

In this style of show, the judging occurs at the exhibit's cage; there is no judging area, enclosure, or ring. The officiating judges work with a moveable table or trolley that is taken to each exhibit's cage. Accompanied by a personal steward, the judge evaluates the exhibit. Awards are marked in the judge's records.

These records, in turn, are sent to a central area, sometimes referred to as the "table", where certificates are completed and awards are allocated. Award stewards place these certificates on the exhibits' cages. When the show is opened to visitors after completion of open class judging, the exhibit's owner returns to the cat's cage to discover which, if any, awards, his cat has earned.

Later in the day, exhibits that have been nominated by the officiating judges as being outstanding examples of their particular breed and color are presented to a panel of judges for their evaluation. The judges then cast written ballots selecting the top winners. This is a very exciting time for all involved and culminates in the selection of the Best in Show winners. Rosettes, trophies and other awards are often presented at this time. Special awards are also announced to the owners and public.

There are a multitude of special awards at some shows including such categories (called side classes) as best eye color, best coat color, best exhibit bred by a member of the licensing club, best imported exhibit, best exhibit bred within a stated distance from the show hall, best debutante, best type, best body, etc. Each of these side classes recognizes specific accomplishments by breeders in producing these beautiful cats. In New Zealand there is a highly-coveted award that recognizes overall merit of cat breeders. This is the "Breeder's Award of Merit". This award is given to a breeder for outstanding achievement. The Breeder's Award of Merit was once awarded to a breeder who produced a new color of Sacred Cat of Burma.

SHOWS IN GREAT BRITAIN

In shows held in Great Britain, the most important classes are those classified as Open. There is an Open class, sub-divided into male and female, for each color and type of Persian recognized for championship status. A few of the colors, such as all the bi-colors, and some of the colorpoints, are grouped together. In these classes, a Persian will compete only against other cats of the same color, except for the grouped colors.

CHALLENGE CERTIFICATES AND GRAND CHALLENGE CERTIFICATES

A challenge certificate is awarded to the winner of the class, provided the judge is of the opinion that the quality is high enough for such an important award. Three of these challenge certificates, from three different judges are required for the cat to gain the coveted title of champion for the rest of its life.

A champion is then eligible to enter the grand champion classes. For Persians these are divided into self-colors and non-self-colors, and again into male and female – a total of four certificates available. In these classes, all Persian colors are grouped together, either self- or non-self colors. The winner of any of these four classes must be an almost-perfect cat, and a splendid specimen of the color and type. Again, three grand challenge certificates, under three different judges are needed before the cat

The Governing Council of the Cat Fancy

GRAND CHALLENGE CERTIFICATE

Pen No.   Name

Show   Date

Signature of Judge

The Governing Council of the Cat Fancy
NEUTER

GRAND PREMIER CERTIFICATE

Pen No.   Name

Show   Date

Signature of Judge

A champion in Great Britain, is elegible to enter the grand champion class-es after earning three challenge certificates. For Persians, a total of four grand champion certificates are available for self-colors, non-self-colors, and male and female.

gains the impressive title of grand champion.

Neutered cats are entered in separate classes. Their top award is a premier certificate, or in the case of grand classes, a grand premier certificate. The same number of wins is needed as for entire cats to gain the title premier or grand premier. At many shows the judge will nominate one adult, one neuter, and one kitten from their open classes to be considered by a small panel of senior judges for best in show award.

MISCELLANEOUS CLASSES

Most shows in Great Britain have a selection of miscellaneous classes in which prize cards and rosettes are awarded. They include the novice class, for exhibits that have not won a first prize in any class at a show held under GCCF rules; limit, for exhibits that have not won more than four first prizes in any class at a show held under GCCF rules; debutante, for exhibits that have never been shown at a GCCF show; maiden, for exhibits that have not won a first, second, or third prize in any class at a GCCF-licensed show; and breeders, for exhibits bred by the exhibitor. This is a fairly wide range of other classes, including club classes, where the exhibitor must be a current member of the club which is named in the class description. It is possible to enter your Persian in a very wide range of classes in the United Kingdom. However, an owner would be wise to limit entry to around four classes. Handling by a large number of stewards and judges may prove very stressful for any cat.

CLEARING THE SHOW HALL

Exhibitors and everybody except judges with their stewards and club officials are barred from the show hall while the Open class is being judged. Judging in the United Kingdom commences at 10 A.M. and the public, that is exhibitors and spectators, are usually allowed back in after mid-day.

AWARDS

Prize cards, and sometimes rosettes are put on the cages by show stewards or club helpers during the course of judging. It is strictly forbidden for anyone to remove these during the course of the day. Challenge certificates, which show the name of the cat are usually not put on the

Rosettes, prize cards, and other awards like these are presented at cat shows in the British Commonwealth.

cage until early in the afternoon when most of the important classes have been judged.

TALKING TO JUDGES

During the course of judging, any conversation between judges, their stewards, and exhibitors is forbidden. However, most judges stroll around the show hall once their judging engagement is complete. This is the time to find them and ask for their opinion of your exhibit. Written reports about the top winners in open classes and miscellaneous classes usually appear in the official journal of the GCCF, *Cats*, about two or three months after a show is held.

FIFE SHOWS

In FIFe shows, cats are evaluated in a judging area. Final awards are determined by a panel of judges after all classes have been completed by each judge. The Best in Show is determined by a panel of judges on the second day of an international show. If it is a one-day show, this will take place at the end of the day.

HOW TO READ THE CATALOG

At shows licensed by the Cat Fanciers' Association in America, the first exhibits listed in the show catalog will be the kittens. Longhair kittens are the first to be listed in the catalog. The longhair kitten entries are followed by shorthair kitten listings. Next in the catalog, information about special exhibits will be listed, including any provisional breeds seeking championship recognition. The next cats listed are the championship longhair exhibits followed by all the championship shorthaired exhibits. Premiership longhair exhibits (neuters and spays) are then followed in the catalog listing by the premiership shorthair exhibits (also neuters and spays). Household cats, non-pedigreed cats, will be listed next in the catalog.

Finally, the listings of all exhibits which are for sale or for exhibition only will appear. Those exhibits which are for sale are available for purchase at the show. "Exhibition only" entries are new breeds of cats, celebrity cats (national winners, famous show cats, or cats that are special in some other way). Cats on exhibition at shows in the United States are sometimes famous mascots in advertising campaigns or cats that have appeared in motion pictures or on television shows. Some may be cats whose owners are celebrities. Others may be performing cats. Animal trainers for the motion picture industry sometimes give demonstrations at the American cat shows showing the training techniques they use for motion pictures.

In Great Britain the catalog order is slightly different. Longhair (Persian) adults are listed first, followed by the kittens, and then the neuters. Somewhere in the catalog will be a list of cats not entered for competition, but shown in exhibition cages. From time to time famous advertising cats or cat personalities from television shows will also be exhibited at British shows. Following the open class listings there will be a fairly substantial section devoted to all the miscellaneous and club classes. All exhibits entered for competition must first be entered in the appropriate open class.

THE BREED STANDARD

In the world of the cat Fancy, the Standard is the absolute authority. It is a meticulously written description of the perfect cat of each breed and color. The Standard is the apex toward which all cat breeders strive. To the degree that any cat does not resemble the written Standard, the cat is said to have faults. For example, if the Standard states that a breed of cat must have round eyes, any eye shape other than round is considered a fault.

The feline associations around the world each have their own accepted Standard of perfection. Each is correct for that country and for the cat Fanciers who exhibit their cats at shows sponsored by that particular association. There are many cat associations in the world. In the United States there are several associations which include the American Cat Association (ACA), American Cat Fanciers' Association (ACFA), the Cat Fanciers' Federation (CFF), and The International Cat Association (TICA). However, the largest American association is CFA, which is also the largest pedigreed cat registry in the world.

In Canada the largest association is the Canadian Cat Association (CCA). In Great Britain, GCCF holds sway with its prestigious history, regulations, judges, and cat exhibitions. An independent group, The Cat Association, was formed some years ago in Great Britain. They also hold cat shows around the country and have recently achieved affiliation with FIFe. In Europe, FIFe is the leading body with member-countries representing most European countries including the Scandinavian countries and England, South America, Mexico, Malaysia, and some of the countries which made up the former Soviet Union. There are a number of large and substantial, independent groups not affiliated with FIFe, in the European countries. Shows under FIFe's patronage are also held in Israel, Latvia, Estonia, Lithuania, Belorussia, the Ukraine, Slovakia, Iceland, Croatia, and Australia. In Australia, each state has its own association, and in New Zealand, there is one major cat association, The New Zealand Cat Fancy, made up of clubs from both the northern and southern islands.

WHAT IS A CAT ASSOCIATION?

Cat associations are founded to achieve specific goals set down in the constitution of each organization. The goals for each are basically the same throughout the world. The constitution of one, for example, lists the following goals:

1. The improvement of the breeds of cats.
2. The promotion of the welfare of all cats.
3. The registration of pedigrees of cats and kittens.
4. The promulgation of rules for the management of cat shows.
5. The licensing of cat shows held under the rules of the organization.
6. The promotion of the interests of breeders and exhibitors of cats.

Each constitution might also include rules for membership in the organization for holding and running meetings, for voting, electing officers, governing rules, rules for discipline, rules for the licensing of shows, provisions for establishing show rules, and rules for licensing judges. These matters are very serious for the cat Fancier since they determine the direction any cat association might take and may determine the appearance of any breed of cat. These organizations with their rules and by-laws find their focus and main activity at each cat show, where evaluations of exhibited cats are carried out. The judges have a lasting effect on the appearance of the pedigreed cat.

WHAT IS A CAT JUDGE?

Each cat association has requirements that judges must meet before being licensed to judge shows. These rules differ among the various associations. Most prospective judges receive detailed and rigorous training before they finally obtain licenses as fully approved judges.

A candidate is required to have, among other things, many years of breeding experience, and experience in raising and successfully exhibiting cats in the category for which the prospective judge plans to train.

Judges, like Will Thompson, pictured here, must have experience in breeding, raising, and successfully exhibiting cats, and knowledge of how a cat show should be run.

Also required is a thorough knowledge of cat shows gained serving as part of show management, the completion of a licensing program, annual written examination in complex clerking skills including the important record-keeping function necessary at all shows, and service in various capacities in a cat club. Additionally, the applicant must have a reputation that will enhance the prestige of the association. A potential judge must command the respect of all who breed and exhibit cats.

In most countries, other than the United States, applicants to the judging program of a cat association must also serve as a steward at shows. This is a difficult task in that a steward must handle many cats during the show for the judges who evaluate the cats. Working as a steward teaches a prospective judge to handle cats and oftentimes requires diplomatic skills.

In Great Britain, cat judges, apart from those working for the Cat Association, are appointed by the GCCF. During the years following World War II, prospective cat judges were recommended to the GCCF by the various breed clubs. Those recommended had acquired skill, knowledge, and success as breeders.

As a result of growing dissatisfaction with this system, representatives of the six oldest, and most important, longhair breed clubs were called to a meeting in 1972 by Dr. Ivor Raleigh, the chairman of the GCCF. He felt that the time had come to regulate the matter of all future judge appointments in the longhair sector of the cat Fancy.

Eric Wickham-Ruffle, an experienced international judge, was the secretary of the GCCF committee for seventeen years, formed to regulate all appointments of judges in the longhair sector of the English cat Fancy.

Eric Wickham-Ruffle was appointed secretary of this body, a post he held until the committee was disbanded seventeen years later. The committee was rapidly expanded, and soon consisted of a total of twenty-nine representatives from all the longhair breed clubs. The judges selection panel was set up by this committee, to consider all future judges' applications. The panel consisted of twelve judges, each qualified for all the longhair lists.

Wide stewarding experience was one of the basic qualifying requirements, and all sensible stewards made a point of stewarding for as many of this distinguished panel of judges as possible. When their applications were considered, most of the panel would thus have thorough and detailed knowledge of the applicants' personal abilities and knowledge.

Some dissatisfaction with the system was expressed in the late eighties, and the advisory committee and judges selection panel were disbanded.

The GCCF set up a committee to consider alternative methods of appointing judges, to be uniform throughout all sectors of the cat Fancy. Cat judges were barred from the committee. A new system was set up in 1990. The judge-recommending groups are now known as BACs (Breed Advisory Committees). Their members are representatives from the various breed clubs, and consist almost entirely of cat breeders, show officials, and others. Very few judges in the longhair sector now sit on these BACs and it was the committee's original idea to bar judges almost entirely. The new system is intended to be more democratic. Whether it will be successful in maintaining the high standards of earlier years remains to be seen. There are many problems, and growing dissatisfaction is being expressed through correspondence in the English cat magazines.

Any prospective judge must possess very special qualities. A judge must not only be a figure who commands respect and authority, but a diplomat, a showman, an expert in handling other people's cats, and, most importantly, a dedicated cat lover. Additionally a judge must have a tremendous depth of knowledge regarding all aspects of breeding, cat genetics, showing, and caring for cats. Additionally, a judge must have the ability to interpret the written Standard.

THE CHALLENGE OF JUDGING

Upon the judges rest the responsibilities for setting the trend, the style, and the realization of perfection in a living animal within the world of the cat Fancy. Cat breeders work with genetic laws of probability and attempt to produce, through careful and studied application of those laws, a living creature whose beauty and temperament might reach the standard of perfection described in the Persian Standard. Judges in the show ring evaluate the success of the breeders in reaching perfection. Perfection very rarely, if ever, is achieved.

Cat judging is not a means of earning a living and most cat judges judge in their spare time, working at a full-time, unrelated profession. In the United States judges are required to undergo an ongoing program of practical training, including attendance at seminars during which breeders and judges discuss the fine points of both new and established breeds. Written examinations are also periodically required. Increasingly, the most experienced and most able judges are sometimes invited to judge at cat shows in other countries.

At any cat show, the expert cat judge must interpret the written Standard as they carefully examine each cat of each breed and each color.

124

Since each cat association throughout the world has its own Standards, judges apply their knowledge and experience to form a mental image of the perfect cat in order to evaluate each cat effectively.

The Persian Standard is a document which describes the ideal Persian pedigreed cat. It is the result of many years of hard work and successes in breeding and showing by breeders who have spent years studying and evaluating the source of the Persian cat's appearance and beauty. The Standard is a definition of beauty. The Standard for the Persian and all other breeds is adjusted, modified, and updated regularly.

In Great Britain any proposed changes to the Standard are discussed initially at the breed club level. Proposed changes are sent to the breed advisory committee, and finally to GCCF for ratification. Once a year in the United States, the members of the CFA breed council, whose members are expert cat breeders, are polled by written ballot regarding proposed modifications to the Standard for their breed. Any change receiving two-thirds of the majority vote is then considered by the association's executive board for formal adoption. Similar reviews of the Standard take place in the other American associations.

GENERAL REQUIREMENTS

One of the earliest requirements for exhibiting cats was the insistence that they be healthy. The health of a cat is still of prime importance in today's shows. If a judge determines that any exhibit is in less than excellent health, that cat is disqualified from all competition at that show. Additionally, not only the cat in question, but all other cats shown by the same exhibitor or agent are required to leave the show hall, as a precaution for other cats. To everyone involved in the cat Fancy the health and safety of these prized animals is always of paramount importance. Many cat shows throughout the world have a vet present to examine every cat before entry is permitted to the show hall to protect the health of all cats at the show. In Great Britain, if something is overlooked and subsequently discovered by a judge, the "duty vet" is called. If he or she agrees with the judge, that cat then must be removed from the show hall immediately.

The next general requirement for showing cats is that all cats must be exhibited in good condition. In general this means that each exhibit must be clean and free of all signs of fleas, dirt, and stains; the exhibit must be of the proper weight in relationship to its size and age; and finally the general appearance, including the coat, must be of good standard and a credit to the breed. If any of these criteria are not met, the judge will withhold all awards from the exhibit. In the United States this is called a "condition withholding" and a judge takes this action if he finds any condition or quality in the cat that in his opinion is temporary in nature.

Finally, exhibits must possess all normal physical characteristics (except in the case of altered, sprayed, or neutered cats) including claws, eyes, ears, legs, tails, etc. Physical characteristics must also be in accordance with the breed Standards. Manx cats, for example, must not have tails.

Regulations describe these important general requirements for any show cat in a series of statements that precede the breed Standards. In a general introduction, CFA, for example, explains the term *condition* as follows: "Condition mirrors the total cat. Diet, care, environment, and heredity all play vital roles in producing a well-conditioned cat; every facet of the cat reflects the results of these important factors." The CFA also requires that a show cat must be in prime condition: faultlessly clean, well-balanced temperamentally, demonstrate "... general health and vigor exhibiting the characteristic grace and beauty natural to the breed ...", and, while handling the cat the judge must evaluate "... the size, shape, bone structure, muscle tone, and basic conformation of the cat ..." that contribute to the "... *total cat* that is equal to the sum of its parts."

ENTERING A SHOW

If you live in the United States, you must obtain an entry form and show announcement for any cat show. You can find listings of coming shows printed in the *Cat Fanciers' Almanac, Cat's Magazine, Cat Fancy Magazine, I Love Cats Magazine* and other magazines published for their members by ACFA and TICA. The listings indicate the date of the shows, the kind of show, its location, names of the officiating judges, and where to get information about the show. If you locate a show you would like to enter, call or write for entry information. Try to apply for entry well in advance of the date of the show. The breeder from whom you purchased your Persian will be happy to help you get started by suggesting shows to attend.

It is important to know that, unless your cat is a kitten (from four months of age up to eight months of age) on the opening day of the show, you will be required to have a registration number issued by the registering body which is licensing the show. Obtaining a registration number normally takes about two to four weeks, assuming that you have the necessary documentation and have included the correct registration fee with your application. You must have this registration number in hand when you appear on the first day of any cat show. The breeder of your Persian is the best person to assist you in registering your cat.

When you receive the entry information, included will be the

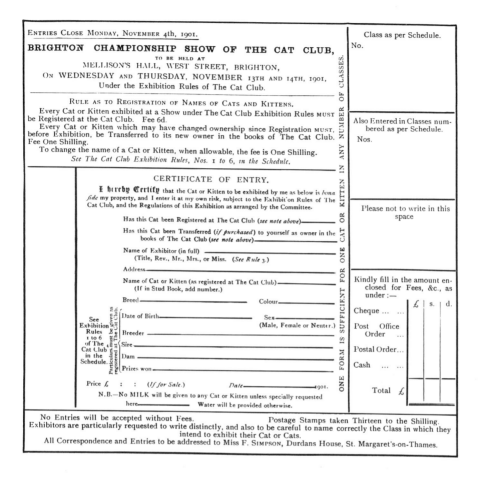

Entries Close Monday, November 4th, 1901.

Class as per Schedule.

No.

BRIGHTON CHAMPIONSHIP SHOW OF THE CAT CLUB,
TO BE HELD AT
MELLISON'S HALL, WEST STREET, BRIGHTON,
On WEDNESDAY and THURSDAY, NOVEMBER 13TH AND 14TH, 1901,
Under the Exhibition Rules of The Cat Club.

RULE AS TO REGISTRATION OF NAMES OF CATS AND KITTENS.

Every Cat or Kitten exhibited at a Show under The Cat Club Exhibition Rules MUST be Registered at the Cat Club. Fee 6d.

Every Cat or Kitten which may have changed ownership since Registration MUST, before Exhibition, be Transferred to its new owner in the books of The Cat Club. Fee One Shilling.

To change the name of a Cat or Kitten, when allowable, the fee is One Shilling.

See The Cat Club Exhibition Rules, Nos. 1 to 6, in the Schedule.

Also Entered in Classes numbered as per Schedule.

Nos.

CERTIFICATE OF ENTRY.

I hereby Certify that the Cat or Kitten to be exhibited by me as below is *bona fide* my property, and I enter it at my own risk, subject to the Exhibition Rules of The Cat Club, and the Regulations of this Exhibition as arranged by the Committee.

Has this Cat been Registered at The Cat Club (*see note above*)———

Has this Cat been Transferred (*if purchased*) to yourself as owner in the books of The Cat Club (*see note above*)———

Name of Exhibitor (in full) ———
(Title, Rev., Mr., Mrs., or Miss. (*See Rule* 3.)

Address———

Name of Cat or Kitten (as registered at The Cat Club)———
(If in Stud Book, add number.)

Breed——— Colour———

Date of Birth——— Sex———
(Male, Female or Neuter.)

Breeder ———

Sire ———

Dam ———

Prizes won———

Price £ : : (*If for Sale.*) Date———1901.

N.B.—No MILK will be given to any Cat or Kitten unless specially requested here——— Water will be provided otherwise.

Please not to write in this space

Kindly fill in the amount enclosed for Fees, &c., as under :—

	£	s.	d.
Cheque			
Post Office Order ...			
Postal Order...			
Cash			
Total £			

ONE FORM IS SUFFICIENT FOR ONE CAT OR KITTEN IN ANY NUMBER OF CLASSES.

See Exhibition Rules 1 to 6 of The Cat Club in the Schedule. Particulars must be given as registered at The Cat Club.

No Entries will be accepted without Fees.

Postage Stamps taken Thirteen to the Shilling.

Exhibitors are particularly requested to write distinctly, and also to be careful to name correctly the Class in which they intend to exhibit their Cat or Cats.

All Correspondence and Entries to be addressed to Miss F. SIMPSON, Durdans House, St. Margaret's-on-Thames.

The requirements to enter the Brighton Championship Show of the Cat Club, held on November 13-14, 1901, are very much the same as today's. The 1901 entry fee was the equivalent of five cents.

address of the show hall, the cage size, the hours of judging during which you and your cat must be present, the number of show rings, and many other details about the show hall and what it provides. In the United States and Canada, the entry information will also indicate that a certain size draperies are required for cages at the show. You may be required to provide a rug, a litter tray for the cage, and food and water dishes. Inoculation and health requirements are also mentioned.

COMPLETING THE ENTRY FORM

The show package you receive will contain an official entry form. Fill out this form and return it with the necessary entry fees as stated in the show announcement. Within a few days, you should receive a confirmation which will tell you whether your entry has been accepted or not. Once accepted, your entry is irrevocable even if you do not attend. If you cannot attend, you must forfeit your entry fee, since the fees are used to defray show expenses including the listing of all cats in the show catalog. If your confirmation has not been received by the Monday preceding the show, call the entry clerk whose name and phone number are included in the show announcement to confirm whether or not your entry has been accepted.

In Great Britain, the routine is slightly different. A list of all the cat shows authorized by the GCCF can be obtained from their office at a cost of £2.00. It would be wise to ask for a copy of the GCCF rules, and the *Guide to Veterinary Defects*. Current prices for these booklets can be checked by telephoning the GCCF office. Ignorance of the rules is not accepted as a reason for breaking them. Armed with these publications, you should be ready to send for a schedule from the show manager. Another source of information on show dates and venues is the official journal, *Cats*. The show schedules are quite explicit and full of helpful information. An entry form will be sent with a schedule. Extracts from the GCCF rules are printed in the schedules and it is wise to read all sections very carefully before submitting your entry. Be sure that your check is made out for the correct fees.

ADVANCE PLANNING

Cat food and cat litter are generally provided by the show producers. However, you may prefer to take your own special brands. Also, if your cat is used to a specific type of water, bring that with you. You will need a grooming kit which contains all the special combs, brushes, and cotton swabs, used at home for grooming. A can opener for cat food and items to clean the wires of the benching cage are good things to remember to pack. Benching cages provided by the show organizers often have grease or other substances on them that can transfer to your Persian's beautifully bathed and groomed coat. You must be sure to prepare for this and many other possible situations at the show. Seasoned exhibitors, including your cat's breeder, can help you to prepare. In fact you can ask to be benched next to someone you know, so that they can help you.

THE FIRST DAY

In the United States when you arrive at the show hall on the open-

Most cat shows have booths set up to sell cat-related items. This comes in handy if grooming tools, litter, or other items are required at a show.

ing day with your cat in a carrier, confirmation of entry, supplies for decorating the cage as well as feeding and grooming, you must first check in with the show secretary. The show secretary is generally near the entrance of the show hall. The show secretary will hand you an envelope containing your exhibitor's badge, your Persian's cage card indicating your cat's catalog number, and a catalog. Often there will be a benching row number included directing you to your cage. You will be shown a diagram or floor plan of the show hall showing the position of every cage. Exhibitor's names are displayed on each cage.

When you find your benching cage, clean and decorate it with draperies and place the rug in the bottom of the cage. Place the filled water dish and litter tray containing litter, into the cage. The benching cage is now ready for your Persian.

The next items are very important. Carefully check the listing in the catalog for your Persian, making sure that all printed information is correct. If the entry is incorrect notify the show secretary or another show official. The listing in the catalog should correspond to the number on your cage card. *This number will serve to identify your Persian for the entire weekend's judging activities.* When it is time for your cat to go to a judging area, this cage and catalog number will be announced over the public address system.

Benching cage requirements for early cat shows were somewhat different from today's. These Persian kitten exhibits were entrants in the 1903 Richmond Cat Show.

Check the judging schedule. This is often printed on the back cover of the catalog. Judging ring numbers are listed for each day. The name of each judge and a list of cats by breed or division in the order they will be judged are also printed. For example, if you are exhibiting a champion adult solid-color Persian, look under each ring for the listing of solid colors in the championship section and circle the listing so you know precisely when your cat will be judged. If your cat is a superior example of solid-color Persian, it might be called back in one or more of the rings for the final awards. Always listen to every announcement carefully for your Persian's number. Don't wait until the last moment to take your cat to the judging ring. Delays please neither fellow exhibitors nor judges. The show is run on a fixed schedule, and unless an announced change is made, the schedule must be adhered to in order to complete all events in good time.

It is helpful to watch each ring to see when the cats just ahead of your Persian are called for judging. When they are called, give your Persian any final grooming touches required so that you can promptly proceed to the judging area when your number is first called.

In Great Britain you will find that all shows, of whatever size, are

Benching cages at American cat shows are often very elaborately decorated.

In the United Kingdom, benching cages generally are unembellished except for rosettes or other awards earned on the day.

held on one day only, and this is always a Saturday. Because of the comparatively small geographical distances involved, the vast majority of exhibitors travel to the show and return on the same day, even though this may involve setting off from home at a very early hour. Very few hotels in Great Britain welcome pets in guest rooms, although occasionally a show schedule will mention one or two which do.

PRELIMINARIES

Before taking your cat to a show, make sure that it has been inoculated at least against Feline Infectious Enteritis and Peritonitis. Take the inoculation certificate with you. Spot checks take place at cat shows and you may be refused entry unless you are able to produce a valid, current certificate. Homeopathic vaccinations are not accepted.

EQUIPMENT

You will need a secure carrying basket or container for your pet, and you must arrive with your Persian in that carrier. As in the United States, there are certain indispensible items of equipment you should bring to a show. You should have a clean cloth and a small bottle of non-toxic disinfectant to wipe out and clean the cage. In the United Kingdom you will need some narrow, white tape to tie a number tag around your Persian's neck. Take a pair of blunt-tipped scissors to cut the tape to the right length. Naturally you will need a comb and a brush, and it would be wise to have a small supply of cotton swabs. You must supply your Persian with a plain, white litter tray, and a supply of a favorite litter. You will also need both a plain, white food dish and water bowl. If you take tinned food, be sure you include a can opener. You will also need a plain, white blanket, one with no distinguishing marks, for the comfort of your cat. Most shows in Great Britain have at least one pet supply stall in case you have forgotten something crucial in the rush to leave home in good time.

In the United Kingdom just before 10 A.M. all exhibitors will be asked over the public address system to leave the hall so that the judges may start their work. Many shows in Great Britain are held in leisure centers or sports centers where you may be able to purchase refreshments in the restaurants. Do not expect gourmet food. Many experienced exhibitors take their own flasks of coffee or tea and their own sandwiches.

DURING JUDGING

In the United States, when your Persian is called for judging and has been placed in the judging cage, it is customary to sit at the front of the judging area to watch the judging. Often the judge will comment about the cats being judged and will point out the good points of each cat.

It is customary to sit at the front of the judging area to watch the judging at American cat shows. Never draw attention to yourself or your cat during judging.

You must never draw attention to yourself or to your cat during judging. There are show rules which cover bad sportsmanship at a show.

At the completion of judging, ribbons will be placed on the judging cages indicating the placement of each cat. When the judge releases the cats, take your Persian plus any ribbons and return to your benching cage. Place your cat back in the cage, hang any award ribbons won on the outside of the cage and wait for your Persian's next call for judging. In American shows, there are generally a total of six or eight judging sessions per breed in a two-day show, which means that your Persian will be evaluated by six or eight different judges. However your cat may only be judged a total of four times in any one day at CFA-sanctioned shows.

After judging, cats are returned to their benching cages. Any awards won are displayed on the benching cages.

At the end of the first day, take your cat home or to a hotel. Many hotels in America allow show cats in their guest rooms. Some exhibitors bring portable cages with them for their cat's protection and comfort in hotel rooms. You will probably choose to do so if you become involved in the fascinating world of the cat Fancy. Remember to check the hotel room completely for hidden problems such as holes in the floor or walls, sharp objects, and places where your Persian might hide and become trapped. Leave the room as clean and odor free as you found it. You should plan your time the next morning so that your cat will be well settled in the benching cage at the opening hour of the show. Do not make the mistake of arriving late in the day if your cat is not scheduled to be judged until early afternoon. Changes in the show schedule often are announced. If your Persian is called to the ring for judging, it is your responsibility to get there even if the published judging schedule may have been changed.

Always remember that a cat show is a spectator event. There will be crowds of visitors at all successful shows. You should plan to be near your Persian at all times during a show. Strange sounds, odors, bright lights, and unfamiliar surroundings can certainly unsettle a cat at the show.

You are the only anchor of security for your Persian. If you have to leave the hall, as is required at shows where the judging is done at the benching cage, stay in the vicinity of the show hall, in case you are needed for an emergency. Be prepared to return to the show hall the moment you are allowed to reenter. At cat shows in Great Britain, although you will be allowed to stay with your Persian after readmission to the hall, you should always move away if a judge approaches your cage.

OUR CATS

AND

ALL ABOUT THEM.

THEIR VARIETIES,
HABITS, AND MANAGEMENT;
AND FOR SHOW,

THE STANDARD OF

EXCELLENCE AND BEAUTY;

DESCRIBED AND PICTURED

BY

HARRISON WEIR, F.R.H.S.

President of " The National Cat Club."

BOSTON AND NEW YORK:
HOUGHTON, MIFFLIN AND COMPANY.
The Riverside Press, Cambridge.
1889.

Harrison Weir published the first feline breed Standards in his book *Our Cats and All About Them.*

CHAPTER VII

THE PERSIAN STANDARD

Harrison Weir, who is considered the father of the cat Fancy, developed the first feline breed Standards as we know them today. By

Manx, or Tailless Cat
British Wild Cat

Persian Cat
English Cat—the Biggest in the Show

Siamese Cats
— French-African Cat

PRIZE CATS

Prize-winning exhibits at the first cat show were sketched by Percy Macquoid for the July 22, 1871 issue of *The Graphic.*

organizing the first cat show, held in London at the Crystal Palace in 1871, he began what has become a worldwide activity.

Harrison Weir is reported to have said, "I conceived the idea that it would be well to hold Cat Shows, so that different breeds, colours, markings, etc., might be more carefully attended to, and the domestic cat sitting

Although the first American cat show was held in New York in 1895, the center of the cat Fancy at the turn of the century was Chicago. Mrs. W. Eames Colburn was one of the most successful cat breeders from this area, shown here with Paris, her famous white, a prolific sire of a long line of champions.

in front of the fire would then possess a beauty and an attractiveness to its owner unobserved and unknown because uncultivated heretofore." Weir decided to organize a cat show, and rapidly worked out a schedule, classes, prices, and prizes. He was the first man to set out "Points of Excellence" or a Standard by which cats could be judged.

THE FIRST CAT SHOWS

The first show was held in the Crystal Palace, a building that was the brainchild of Prince Albert, the consort of Queen Victoria. It was built almost entirely of glass. The first modern cat show was held on July 13, 1871, and there were approximately 160 exhibits. John Jennings in his book *Domestic or Fancy Cats,* written in 1895 said, "Many will remember the sensation created by this first Cat Exhibition, which opened up a channel for the feline race never hitherto dreamt of." This first modern cat show proved to be the forerunner of cat shows throughout the world today, and marked the beginning of the cat Fancy.

In 1875 a show was held in Edinburgh which attracted an entry of no less than 560 cats. Cat shows became very popular in the United Kingdom, particularly as they were patronized by Queen Victoria.

At the first cat show held in London at the Crystal Palace, the exhibits were led, or "dragged," it was reported, on leashes. This practice oftentimes led to much excitement when two tom cats came into fighting distance.

Judges at work at the Richmond Cat Show at the turn of the century.

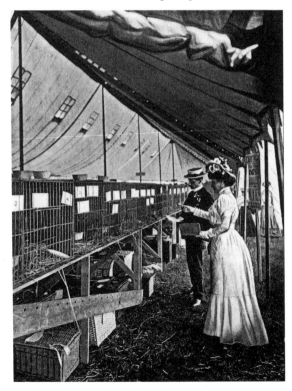

This blue Persian was presented to Queen Victoria by Miss Patterson, a breeder of blues who was a member of the first committee of the Blue Persian Cat Society, founded in England on April 24, 1901.

EARLY CAT CLUBS

In London the National Cat Club was formed in 1887 with Harrison Weir as its first president. It became the first registering body for pedigreed cats in the world. The National Cat Club started the practice of keeping stud books, records of all cats gaining prizes at shows. It continued with this foundation work until 1910, when the Governing Council of

The Cat Club medal was designed by Mrs. Paul Hardy, a well-known breeder of blues in the early 1900s. It was awarded in silver and bronze at the annual Westminster show in London.

County fairs were where the first American cat shows were held at the turn of the century, much in the spirit of this show at Richmond near London, held out-of-doors.

the Cat Fancy took over this function.

In 1901 the Red, Cream, and Tortie Cat Society was started in the United Kingdom and in the decades since, it has had many distinguished presidents. Eric Wickham-Ruffle has been the president of the club for many years. Another of the very old breed clubs in Great Britain is the Blue Persian Cat Society, also founded in 1901.

In the United States, in the late 1800s, local cat exhibitions were held at county fairs. The first official cat show in the United States was held in New York City at Madison Square Garden on May 8, 1895. This led to the founding of the first cat clubs in the United States and the creation of American cat associations. These associations registered cats, wrote formal Standards, and licensed cat shows. Those early Standards have been modified to reflect the changing ideas of perfection.

THE PERFECT PERSIAN

The Persian Standard is one of the most stable of all Standards in the cat Fancy. Except for additions of new colors and slight changes to color descriptions, it has largely survived as Harrison Weir first described the Persian at the turn of the century. The Persian Standard describes the perfect Persian. If a particularly stylish attribute is not described in the Standard, that feature is considered undesirable. This basic rule is followed by most cat organizations throughout the world. Most judges will agree that they have never found a perfect cat of any breed, although some cats on the international show bench do approach perfection.

THE POINT SYSTEM

Today's Persian Standard allocates a 100-point total score for a Persian, perfect in every detail. For the Persian breed and all others, each feature is allocated a proportion of the total points. The point breakdown is a quick indicator of which features of a breed the judges and breeders consider most important, for perfection in these categories is difficult to achieve. For example, in the United States, the number of total points that can be earned by a Persian for perfect coat color is twenty, but the total number that can be earned for coat color by the Devon Rex is only five.

In Great Britain, the number of points a Persian or longhair can earn for coat color varies according to the color. Chinchillas, for instance, are allocated twenty-five total points, pewters thirty points, and in other colors, texture, evenness of color, quality of coat and markings are assigned the higher score of forty points for perfection.

Persians, in American associations of all colors and patterns, are judged by one set of points indicated below. *

HEAD	(Including size and shape of eyes, ear shape and set):	30 points
TYPE	(Including shape, size bone, and length of tail):	20 points
COAT:		10 points
BALANCE:		5 points
REFINEMENT:		5 points
COLOR:		20 points
EYE COLOR:		10 points
TOTAL:		100 points

* The Standard as printed here, courtesy of the Cat Fanciers Association, Inc.

In all tabby varieties, the twenty points designated for color are divided into ten for markings and ten for color. In all "with white" varieties (calico, dilute-calico, bi-color, van-bi-color, van-calico, van-dilute-calico, and tabby-and-white), the twenty points designated for color are divided into ten for "with white" pattern and ten for color.

Standards in Great Britain and the British Commonwealth member countries are often structured to treat each Persian color, or group of colors, as a separate breed. Points allocated vary slightly from group to group. The GCCF Standard assigns forty points for coat (including the color, texture and quality, and unevenness of color of the coat) for the solid colors. For Chinchillas, the color accounts for twenty-five points of the total score, with fifteen points allocated for coat and condition. In pewters, coat and condition together are assigned a perfect score of ten points, with a further thirty assigned for perfection of color. For color-points, coat (including color, texture, markings, etc.) is allocated a total of twenty-five points. The FIFe Standard is much easier to memorize as a uniform allocation of points is made for all Persians.

DISQUALIFICATION

Disqualification is the most serious penalty the judge may invoke in the show ring. Judges may disqualify a cat if it acts in a threatening or intractable manner. Fanciers must breed cats for conformation or beauty, but a good temperament is equally important. Judges may also disqualify any entry showing excessive use of white or other colored powder, tints or color rinses, or any other artificial tampering with the natural coat color. The plucking of button and locket markings and the use of drugs to alter the temperament are all disqualifying factors.

Most cat associations have a list of disqualification points which apply to the Persian, as follows:

1. A locket or pure white area under the chin, or a button, an area of white generally found in the groin area or under the arms, when white is not part of the cat's general color, is reason for disqualification.
2. Bone deformities, abrupt angle changes in the tail's natural and expected direction, lumps of cartilage or calcium deposits in the tail bone are features for which a cat will be disqualified.
3. A Persian must have five toes on each front paw and four on each rear paw.
4. A weakness in the hind quarters, incorrect bone structure in the rear legs, and deformity of the spine are disqualifying factors.
5. Skull deformities resulting in an assymetrical face and/or head, a crooked jaw, or muzzle, crossed eyes, one eye larger or set higher in the head than the other, or nose leather set at an improper angle are all reasons for disqualification.
6. Pointed Persians must not have white toes or eye color other than blue.
7. The Chinchilla, shaded-silver, and shaded-golden will be disqualified for any eye color other than green or blue-green.

The GCCF includes a list of withholding faults in the preface to the Persian Standard. These include depressions or protrusions in the skull; reduced nostril aperture; exaggerated depression of the nasal bridge or stop; permanent squint (strabismus); incorrect dentition; kinks in the spine or tail; and abnormal number of toes. Adult cats and kittens showing any of these faults will not be awarded first prizes and no certificate will be awarded to an adult. The FIFe Standards include most of these withholding faults and in addition lists others, such as undernourishment, obesity, blindness, eye damage, and declawed cats.

BALANCE

All Persian Standards begin with a description of the perfect Persian cat in similar, general terms. The Standard states that, "... the ideal Persian should present an impression of a heavily-boned, well-balanced cat with a sweet expression and soft, round lines. The large round eyes set wide apart in a large round head contribute to the overall appearance." The head must be the proper size in relation to the cat's length and width. The tail must be neither too long nor short. All features must be in proportion.

REFINEMENT

Refinement is perhaps the most abstract part of any judge's evaluation of a Persian or cat of any breed. Refinement refers to the overall impression the cat gives to the trained eye of the judge. It is the total sum of all the elements that make up a cat. A Persian, for instance, must not be gross in appearance or too light and lacking in substance of appearance. It is refinement which a judge looks for which differentiates a very good Persian from a beautiful one. It could best be described, perhaps, as star quality.

IMPORTANT FEATURES

The head must be, "...round and massive, with great breadth of skull." (TICA's Standard indicates that the head should be "medium to large.") The face should be "...round with round underlying bone structure" (CFF requires that "...the full face should appear to be square.") The Persian's head must be "...well set on a short, thick neck." The GCCF Standard is almost exactly the same. Some judges and breeders find it helpful to picture the head as a large sphere in correct proportion, with the heavy-boned body. A short, thick neck is required.

The nose must be short, snub, and broad, with the break centered between the eyes. ACFA's Standard indicates that the nose should be "... as broad as it is long." The break is an indentation in the skull located just above the nose leather of the Persian between the eyes. Old photographs of Persians reveal that the cats of the turn of the century totally lacked any nose break. It is the break that gives some of today's Persians a snub-nosed profile. It is important to note that in Great Britain it is a withholding fault if the upper edge of the nose leather is above the lower edge of the eye.

Crystal, a blue-eyed white Champion of 1903, (left) totally lacked any nose break, as compared to this photo below of Gr. Ch. Windibank Patti-Kake of Azulita, an orange-eyed white champion of the 1950s.

The cheeks must be full, and the jaws broad and powerful. The CFF Standard, in more detail, indicates that the cheeks should give "...the impression of a shallow furrow starting from the inner corner of the eye and gently curving downward toward the outer corner of the lip line, giving the appearance of a sloping mustache." The chin must be "...full, well-developed, and firmly rounded, reflecting a proper bite." The ears must be "...small, round tipped, tilted forward, and not unduly open at the base; they are set far apart, and low on the head, fitting into (without distorting) the rounded contour of the head." The eyes should be "...brilliant in color, large, round, and full..." and "...set level and far apart, giving a sweet expression to the face." The GCCF and FIFe General Type Standards for Persians basically agree with the general description of the breed, however FIFe gives greater detail.

FIFe requires that the head be "...round and massive with great breadth of skull; well-balanced. Full cheeks, round forehead. Short, broad nose with stop; the stop to be between the eyes, not above the upper eyelid or below the lower eyelid. Small, round-tipped ears, set wide apart and low on the head, with full ear tufts. Strong chin. Broad and powerful jaws." The excellent description of the placement of the break or stop is an improvement on the American description in that it clearly indicates that it is the break that determines the placement of the nose in relation to the other features in the head.

The GCCF Standards were revised in September 1992. For self-colored Persians the wording is somewhat similar to that of the FIFe Standard except that no precise definition of the break (stop) is given. Perhaps the longest description is for colorpoints, where a "...short broad nose of even width with stop..." is required. The tabby Standard mentions a stop that is "not extreme". For the other colors there is a description of "snub nose" or "broad snub nose". It is interesting that this basic definition of one feature of the Persian's facial structure has brought about great controversy between those Fanciers who choose to follow the CFA's description of the extreme-type and those who find a more natural beauty in the more traditional-type Persian.

The large, brilliantly-colored eyes of the Persian give an openness to its countenance which most people find very appealing. Envision a cat with these large, colorful eyes; short, snub nose; and small, round-tipped ears, and you have a picture of the type of Persian that is prevalent on the international show bench today. By snubbing the nose and placing it in the head so that it is nearly even with a line draw through the center of the eyes, breeders have produced the extreme-type or modern-type Persian of the American show bench, as opposed to the more moderate, traditional-type Persian.

American Standards require that the Persian's body must be of "...cobby type low on the legs, broad and deep through the chest, equally massive across the shoulders and rump, a well-rounded mid section and level back." CFF's Standard indicates that, "The rump of the female tends to be rounder than that of the male." The Persian must also have "...good muscle tone with no evidence of obesity." The Persian should never be a small cat but must be either large or medium in size, however, quality is the real determining factor and not size. The FIFe and GCCF size Standards are very similar to those of the American cat associations.

THE PERSIAN COAT

The CFA Standards require that the perfect coat be "...long and thick, standing off from the body, of fine texture, glossy and full of life, long all over the body, including the shoulders." The ACA, CFF, and TICA Standards point out that "allowances should be made for seasonal

At its best, the tail hair of the Persian produces a brush as wide as the cat's body when it is in full coat.

148

variations in length and thickness." CFF's Standard further indicates: "There are two types of Persian coats allowable—long and flowing, or medium long and thick."

CFA requires that the ruff should be "...immense and continuing in a deep frill between the front legs. Ear and toe tufts long. Brush very full." The beautiful and fully-coated tail of the cat is the brush. The tail hair of the Persian, when at its best, produces a brush as wide as the cat's fully-coated body.

THE PERSIAN COLORS

Because there are so many different colors and because of the great numbers of Persians entered in shows compared with other breeds, American cat associations group breed colors and patterns by coat differences or patterns. This system makes the mechanics of determining awards more logical and equitable.

The system divides Persians and other breeds into divisions. The system adopted in America categorizes Persians into the following divisions:

1. The solid-color divisions for all cats with coats of one color.
2. The shaded division for cats with coats tipped with color.
3. The smoke division for cats with coats that are solid in color but with a contrasting undercoat color due to the depth and amount of tipping.
4. The tabby division for cats with classic (blotched) or mackerel-tabby patterned coats.
5. The parti-color division for those cats with blue-cream or tortoiseshell coats.
6. The bi-color division for cats with coat color of white along with a recognized solid, tabby pattern, multi-color (such as the calico and dilute calico), or smoke portions of color arranged in specific proportions and styles. This category includes both the bi-color and van bi-color cat.
7. The Himalayan division for pointed Persians.

These divisions apply only to the United States. In Great Britain and Europe every individual color of Persian is judged in its own class. This means that a Persian or any breed is judged against cats of the same color.

THE SOLID COLOR PERSIAN

The solid color Persians are always outstanding in type and presentation. Their one-colored (self-colored) coats make them very eye-catching and spectacular at any show. The blue-eyed white is always popular, and many of today's black Persians come very close to attaining the perfection described in the Standards. A copper-eyed or blue-eyed white Persian is always outstanding. The blues, reds, creams, chocolates, and lilacs add to this flower garden of colors.

The white Persian must be "Pure glistening white. Nose leather and paw pads: pink. Eye color: deep blue and brilliant copper." The odd-eyed white Standard requires that "odd-eyed whites shall have one blue and one copper eye with equal color depth." For many years there was a show rule which required that any odd-eyed white Persian with a spot of blue in the copper or copper in the blue eye be disqualified. CFA

This is the original Standard Harrison Weir wrote for the white Persian. He also sketched his choice of a near-perfect speciman of this color.

has dropped the rule and the Standard for the odd-eyed white does not contain this disqualification. The GCCF Standard, however withholds certificates for flecks or traces of incorrect color in either iris in all the Persian colors. The GCCF Standard for self-color cats requires copper or deep orange eyes.

THE BLUE PERSIAN CAT SOCIETY PEDIGREE FORM.

Breed and Sex_____   Breeder_____

Colour_____   Date of Birth _____

Name of Cat _____

PARENTS.	GRAND-PARENTS.	GREAT GRAND-PARENTS.	GREAT GREAT GRAND-PARENTS.
Sire.			*ex*
			ex
			ex
			ex
Dam.			*ex*
			ex
			ex
			ex

Prizes Won, Remarks, &c._____

These Forms, at 8d. per dozen, can be obtained on application to Miss F. Simpson, Hon. Sec., 9, Leonard Place, Kensington, W.

The Blue Persian Cat Society pedigree form of 1903.

The blue Persian must be "...blue, lighter shades preferred, one level tone from nose to tip of tail. Sound to the roots. A sound, darker shade is more acceptable than an unsound, lighter shade." Nose leather and paw pads must be blue and the eye color must be a brilliant copper. The GCCF asks for medium to pale blue coat color.

The black Persian must be lustrous, "...dense coal black and sound from roots to tip of the fur; free from any tinge of rust on tips or smoke undercoat. Nose leather: black. Paw pads: black or brown." Eye color must be copper or deep orange.

The red Persian's color is "...deep, rich, clear, brilliant red; without shading, markings or ticking." The nose leather and paw pads must be pink and the eye color brilliant copper in color, as described by the CFA

The red Persian's color is "...deep, rich, clear, brilliant red; without shading, markings or ticking." The nose leather and paw pads must be pink and the eye color brilliant copper in color, as described by the CFA Standard. The color for the peke-faced red is the same.

The cream Persian must have a coat color of "...one level shade of buff cream, without markings. Sound to the roots. Lighter shades preferred." The nose leather and paw pads should be pink and the eye color a brilliant copper. The GCCF stipulates a pale to medium-cream coat color.

The "other solid colors" class consists of two colors: self-chocolate and self-lilac. (ACFA calls this color frost). These colors are judged together as a single class. The chocolate must be a rich, warm, chocolate-brown, sound from the roots to the tip of fur, have brown nose leather and paw pads, and brilliant, copper eye color. This lovely color and the lilac color are by-products of the careful breeding which took place to produce the Himalayan Persians. The lilac must be a rich, warm lavender with a pinkish tone, sound and even throughout. The nose leather and paw pads must be pink. The eye color must be brilliant copper. Under GCCF rules the chocolate and lilac color have individual classes.

This 1903 photo of the "perfect" Chinchilla shows a cat which is quite different from the Standard for this color on today's show bench.

THE SHADED DIVISION

The shaded division contains some of the most beautiful of all Persians. In fact, photographers often use the Chinchilla or shaded

One of the most famous of Chinchillas, bred by Eric Wickham-Ruffle, was the real star of a James Bond movie.

Persians as models for advertisements in which a gorgeous cat is required. In Great Britain one of the most famous advertising cats was the Kosset Carpet cat, a lovely male Chinchilla (sadly now deceased) which lived with Rosemary Gowdy, one of the senior GCCF Persian judges and a highly successful breeder of Chinchillas. When photographed, the black tipping of the Chinchilla-silver Persian's coat disappears resulting in what appears to be a beautiful, angelic white cat. Couple this with the fact that the silver Persian has natural mascara around each eye and around the margin of the nose, and you have a photographer's dream. The deep, emerald-green or blue-green eye color adds the final touch.

The color for the silver Persian's coat is produced a little different-ly than those of solid-color Persians. Each hair shaft of the silver's coat is translucent whereas each hair shaft of a solid-color is opaque, filled with color-producing factors. It is this translucence that gives the sparkling appearance to the silver's coat.

The golden Persian has a rich, warm, brownish-sienna-toned

undercoat with black tipping and jade green eyes. The GCCF description of color is "...undercoat apricot deepening to gold."

The cameo Persian is very reminiscent of the beautiful Italian cameo broaches which were very popular in England and America at the turn of the century. These cats, with their white undercoat and red-cream tipping are required by the Standard to have brilliant copper or deep orange eyes.

In Great Britain the pewter Persian is recognized. In most respects this color is very similar to the shaded-silver. The important factor is that unlike the other silver cats in Great Britain, the pewter does not have green, but orange or copper eyes. Any trace of green is considered a fault.

Completing the shaded division colors are the shells and shaded-tortoiseshells that are very much like the silvers except they have distinct red-and-cream-tipped patches to set off their brilliant, copper eyes. These are beautiful cats that have black, red, and cream overtones on a light ground color of undercoat.

The Chinchilla-silver has an undercoat of pure white. The coat on the back, flanks, head, and tail is sufficiently tipped with black to give the characteristic sparkling silver appearance; the legs may be slightly shaded with tipping. The chin, ear tufts, stomach, and chest must be pure white; and the rims of the eyes, the lips, and the nose outlined with black. The eye color must be green or blue-green. Chinchilla-silvers with eye color other than green or blue-green are disqualified.

The shaded-silver in the United States has an undercoat of white with a mantle of black tipping shading down the sides of the body, face, and tail and changing from being dark on the ridge, to white on the chin, chest, stomach, and under the tail. The legs must be the same tone as the face. The general effect is of a cat that is much darker than a Chinchilla. The rims of the eyes, the lips, and the nose should be outlined with black. The nose leather must be brick-red and the paw pads must be black. The eye color must be green or blue-green. Shaded-silvers must have green or blue-green eye color.

The shell-cameo (red-Chinchilla) in the United States has an undercoat of white with the coat on the back, flanks, head, and tail sufficiently tipped with red to give the characteristic sparkling appearance. The face and legs may be very slightly shaded with tipping, while the chin, ear tufts, stomach, and chest must be white. The nose leather, rims of the eyes, and the paw pads must be rose-colored, while the eye color must be brilliant copper.

The shaded-cameo (red-shaded) in the United States, has an undercoat of white with a mantle of red tipping shading down the sides, face, and tail. The shading should be dark on the ridge and white on the chin, chest, stomach, and under the tail. The legs must be the same tone as the face. The general effect is much redder than the shell-cameo. The nose leather, rims of the eyes, and paw pads must be rose-colored, while the eye color must be brilliant copper.

The Chinchilla-golden in the United States has an undercoat color of rich, warm cream. The coat on the cat's back, flanks, head, and tail must be sufficiently tipped with black so as to give a golden appearance. The legs of the Chinchilla-golden may be slightly shaded with tipping, and the chin, ear tufts, stomach, and chest must be cream-colored. The rims of the eyes, lips, and nose must be outlined with black. The nose leather color must be deep rose and the paw pads black. The eye color must be green or blue-green.

In America the shaded-golden has an undercoat of rich, warm cream. A mantle of black tipping should shade down the sides, face, tail, and be dark on the ridge and cream on the chin, chest, stomach, and under the tail. The legs must be the same tone as the face. The general effect is much darker than a Chinchilla-golden. The rims of the eyes, the lips, and the nose must be outlined with black. The nose leather color must be deep rose, and the paw pads must be black. The eye color must be green or blue-green. In Great Britain, there is no distinction between the Chinchilla-golden and shaded-golden and color is referred to as golden. The undercoat must be apricot deepening to gold. The mantle may be any shade of gold, tipped with seal, brown, or black.

The shell-tortoiseshell has a white undercoat; the coat on the back, flanks, head, and tail must be delicately tipped in black with well-defined patches of red-and cream-tipped hairs just as in the pattern of the tortoiseshell. The cat's face and legs may be slightly shaded with tipping while the chin, ear tufts, stomach, and chest must be white to very slightly tipped. A blaze of red or cream tipping on the face is desirable, and the eye color must be brilliant copper.

The shaded-tortoiseshell has an undercoat of white, covered with a mantle of black tipping, and clearly defined patches of red-and-cream-tipped hairs as in the pattern of the tortoiseshell. There should be shading down the sides, face, and tail from the legs, and under the tail. The general effect must be much darker than the shell-tortoiseshell. A blaze of red or cream tipping on the face is desirable. The eye color must be brilliant copper. The GCCF descriptions for the cameo are quite similar to the shaded-tortoiseshell description and recognize this color in the shell and shaded intensities, and in red, tortie, cream, and blue-cream. The tortie-cameos should have patched color, whereas the blue-cream cameo should have the tipping softly intermingled.

THE SMOKE DIVISION

Perhaps the most striking of all Persian color is the smoke division. These cats appear to be black, blue, cream, red, tortoiseshell, or blue-cream until they move or until their coat is parted. The contrasting undercoat transforms the entire cat into a swath of silk moire. All have brilliant, copper eye color. The beautiful coats are quite fragile in that dampness, light, and seasonal changes are all very tough on the color. The ruff, or frill, is also fragile. A smoke will generally be in good coat for about eight to ten weeks of the year. This is a period of true glory, but the smoke is still a very striking Persian when not in full coat.

The black-smoke Persian has a white undercoat which is deeply tipped with black. The cat in repose appears black and when in motion, the white undercoat is clearly apparent. The points and mask must be black with a narrow band of white at the base of the hairs next to the skin and should be seen only when the fur is parted. Black-smokes have a light silver frill and ear tufts. The nose leather and paw pads must be black and the eye color brilliant copper.

The blue-smoke Persian has a white undercoat which is deeply tipped with blue. While in repose, the cat appears to be blue, but when it is in motion, the cat's undercoat is clearly apparent. The points and mask must be blue with a narrow band of white at the base of the hairs next to the skin which should be seen only when the fur is parted. Blue-smokes must have a white frill and ear tufts. The nose leather and paw pads must be blue in color. The eye color must be brilliant copper.

The cream-smoke Persian has a white undercoat deeply tipped with cream. While in repose, the cat should appear to be cream, but, when moving, the cat's white undercoat should be clearly apparent. The points and mask must be cream with a narrow band of white at the base of the hairs next to the skin and should be seen only when the fur is parted. Cream-smokes must have a white frill and ear tufts, and nose leather and paw pads of pink. Eye color must be brilliant copper.

The cameo-smoke (red-smoke) has a white undercoat which is deeply tipped with red. In repose, the cat must appear to be red, and when in motion, the white undercoat should be clearly apparent. The points and mask must be red with a narrow band of white at the base of the hairs next to the skin to be seen only when the fur is parted. They must have a white frill and ear tufts and the nose leather, rims of the eyes, and paw pads must be rose-colored. The eye color should be brilliant copper.

The smoke-tortoiseshell has a white undercoat that is deeply tipped with black, with clearly-defined, unbridled patches of red-and-cream-tipped hairs as in the pattern of the tortoiseshell. In repose, the cat should appear to be tortoiseshell, but while in motion, the white undercoat should be clearly apparent. The face and ears must display the tortoise-shell pattern, with a narrow band of white at the base of the hairs next to the skin, to be seen only when the fur is parted. They must have a white ruff and ear tufts. A blaze of red or cream tipping on the face is desirable and the eye color must be brilliant copper.

The blue-cream smoke has a white undercoat deeply tipped with blue and with clearly-defined patches of cream as in the pattern of the blue-cream. The GCCF requires the blue-and-cream to be softly intermingled. The cat, when in repose, should appear to be blue-cream, but while in motion, the cat's white undercoat must be clearly apparent. The face and ears must have the blue-cream pattern but with a narrow band of white at the base of the hair next to the skin to be seen only when the fur is parted.

The frown marks on the forehead of the classic tabby should form an intricate letter M.

They must have a white ruff and ear tufts. A blaze of cream tipping on the face is desirable and the eye color must be brilliant copper. The FIFe Standard allows for either patched or intermingled colors. GCCF also recognizes chocolate-smokes, lilac-smokes, chocolate-tortie-smokes, and lilac-tortie-smokes.

THE TABBY PATTERNS

The tabby Persians present a contrast of an intricate, darker pattern against a complimentary, lighter, ground. They are recognized in two distinct patterns. The classic or blotched tabby pattern has a distinctive bull's eye marking in the center of each of the cat's sides and the mackerel-tabby has a pattern of thin penciling often resembling the clouds of a buttermilk sky.

In the classic tabby-pattern - the only *pattern* accepted to date for Persians by GCCF – the markings are dense, clearly defined, and broad. The legs should be evenly barred with bracelets that come up to meet the body markings, and the tail must be evenly ringed. There must be several unbroken necklaces on the neck and upper chest, the more the better. Frown marks on the forehead should form an intricate letter M. An unbroken line should run back from the outer corner of the eye, and there must be swirls on the cheeks. Vertical lines over the back of the head should extend to the cat's shoulder-markings, shaped like a butterfly, with both upper and lower wings distinctly outlined and marked with dots inside the outline. The back's markings should consist of a vertical line down the spine, from butterfly to tail, with a vertical stripe paralleling it on each side. The three stripes should be well-separated by stripes of the ground color. A large, solid blotch on each side of the cat's body should be encircled by one or more unbroken rings, and these side markings should be the same on both sides. There should be double vertical rows of buttons on the chest and stomach. GCCF requires that the abdominal area be spotted. CFA requires that eye color for all tabby Persians must be brilliant copper for all colors except the silver-tabby which may have brilliant copper, hazel or green eyes. GCCF requires that the silver-tabby have eyes of green or hazel; brown or red-tabbies should have orange or copper eyes; blue tabbies must have hazel or copper eyes.

In the mackerel-tabby pattern, the markings are dense, clearly defined, and made up of narrow penciling. The legs must be evenly barred with narrow bracelets coming up to meet the body markings; the tail must also be barred. The neck and chest must have distinct necklaces.

The head must be barred with an M on the forehead. Unbroken lines must run back from the eyes, and lines must run down the head to meet the shoulder. The spine lines must run together to form a narrow saddle. Narrowing penciling should run around the body.

The patched-tabby pattern (torbie pattern) is an established silver, brown, or blue tabby with patches of red and/or cream. The established tabby patterns are classic or mackerel.

THE TABBY DIVISION

The tabby division's cats are intricately patterned. All may have brilliant copper eye color. In addition, the silver tabby may have green, hazel, or copper eye color, while the silver-patched tabby's eyes can be hazel or copper colored. In the United Kingdom eye color for silver-patched tabbies must be green or hazel.

The silver tabby (classic, mackerel) has a ground color (including the lips and chin) of pale, clear silver; the markings must be dense black. The nose leather must be brick-red, the paw pads black, and the eye color must be green, brilliant copper, or hazel. In Great Britain copper eyes are a fault.

The silver-patched tabby (torbie-classic or -mackerel) has a ground color (including the lips and chin) of silver with classic or mackerel-tabby markings of dense black, with patches of red and/or cream, clearly defined on both body and extremities. A blaze of red and/or cream on the face is desirable. The eye color must be either brilliant copper or hazel.

The red tabby (classic, mackerel) has a ground color of red; the markings are a deep, rich red, and the lips and chin must also be red. The nose leather and paw pads must be brick-red and the eye color, brilliant copper. The color for the peke-faced-red tabby is the same.

The brown tabby (classic, mackerel) has a ground color of brilliant, coppery brown with markings of dense black. The lips and chin must be the same shade as the rings around the eyes. The back of the leg must be black from the paw to the heel. The nose leather must be brick-red and the paw pads, black or brown. The eye color must be brilliant copper.

The brown-patched tabby has a ground color which is a brilliant copper-brown with the classic or mackerel-tabby markings made up of dense black with patches of red and/or cream, clearly defined on both body and extremities. A blaze of red and/or cream on the face is desirable. The lips and chin must be the same shade as the rings around the eyes; the eye color must be brilliant copper.

The blue tabby (classic, mackerel) has a ground color (including the lips and the chin) of pale, bluish-ivory; the markings are a very deep blue affording a good contrast with the ground color. The coat should have warm fawn overtones or an overall patina. The nose leather must be old rose, the paw pads must be rose-colored, and the eye color must be brilliant copper.

The blue-patched tabby (torbie-classic or -mackerel) has a ground color (including the lips and chin) of pale bluish-ivory with deep blue classic or mackerel tabby markings providing good contrast to the ground color. Patches of cream must be clearly defined on both the body and the extremities; a blaze of cream on the face is desirable. The coat must have warm fawn overtones or an overall patina. The eye color must be brilliant copper. A cat lacking the rich, warm patina overall is defined by CFA as a pewter tabby and is not currently recognized by CFA.

The cream tabby (classic, mackerel) has a ground color (including the lips and the chin) of very pale cream with markings of buff or cream sufficiently darker than the ground color. The markings should provide good contrast but remain within the dilute color range. The nose leather and paw pads must be pink; the eye color must be brilliant copper.

The cameo tabby (classic, mackerel) has a ground color which is off-white; the markings are red. The nose leather and paw pads must be rose-colored and the eye color a brilliant copper. All cameo tabby colors, should have orange or copper eyes.

The GCCF has given preliminary recognition to several other tabby colors. There is the chocolate tabby which has rich, chocolate-brown markings on a bronze-agouti ground color; the lilac tabby with lilac markings on a beige-agouti ground; the tortie tabby; the blue tortie-tabby; the chocolate-tortie tabby; and the lilac-tortie tabby. In all these colors, the tabby patterns are overlaid with shades of the other color. In America the chocolate-tortoiseshell and the lilac-cream Persians are judged against each other in the "other parti-colors" class.

PARTI-COLOR DIVISION

The parti-color division consists of multi-colored cats whose colors do not include white. These have patterned black coats with unbrindled red-and-cream patching or pale blue patching with ample cream. For blue creams the GCCF requires the two colors, cream and blue,

Copper-eyed white

Blue-eyed white, bred in England

Black

Black, bred in England

Blue, bred in England

Red

Red, bred in England

Cream, bred in England

Shaded Silver

Golden, bred in England

Shaded-Cameo

Chinchilla Silver

Black Smoke

Black Smoke, bred in England

Blue-Cream Smoke, bred in England

Silver Tabby, bred in England

Brown Tabby

Brown Classic Tabby, bred in England

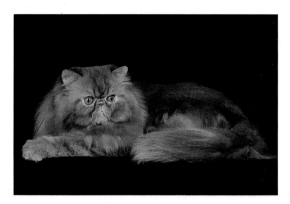

Red Tabby

Red Classic Tabby, bred in England

Brown-Patched Tabby

Blue Mackerel Tabby

Tortoiseshell

Tortoiseshell, bred in England

Blue-Cream Parti-Color

Cream-and-White Bi-Color

Red-and-White Bi-Color, bred in England

Blue-and-White Van Bi-Color

Seal-Point Himalayan

Flame-Point Himalayan

Blue-Point Colorpoint, bred in England

Blue-Point Himalayan

Cream-Point Himalayan

Cream-Point Colorpoint, bred in England

to be softly intermingled and pastel in tone. These cats are almost always females. On occasion a parti-color male will appear; generally these males are sterile.

The tortoiseshell in the United States is basically a black cat with unbrindled patches of red and cream in the coat. The GCCF describes the patching colors as shades of red. These patches must be defined and well-broken on both the body and extremities; a blaze of red or cream on the face is desirable. The eye color must be brilliant copper.

The blue-cream is a blue cat with patches of solid cream. CFA requires the patches to be clearly defined and well-broken on both the body and its extremities. FIFe allows both. The eye color must be brilliant copper.

The chocolate-tortoiseshell is a rich, warm chocolate-brown cat with patches of red. The patches must be clearly defined and well-broken both on the body and extremities. The nose leather and paw pads must be brown and/or brick red. The eye color must be brilliant copper.

The lilac-cream is a rich, warm, pinkish-toned, lavender cat with patches of cream. The patches must be clearly defined and well-broken on both the body and extremities. The nose leather and paw pads must be pink in color. The eye color must be brilliant copper. The GCCF requires these colors to be pastel in tone and softly intermingled.

BI-COLOR DIVISION

Some of the most spectacular of all Persians are in the bi-color division. The bi-colors can be two- and three-colored cats; white is counted as a color. As with the tortoiseshell and blue-creams, the calico and patched-tabby-and-whites are almost always females. On the occasion when a male does appear, he is most often sterile. Nature seems to reserve many-colored coats for the female of the species. As a minimum requirement a bi-color should have white feet, legs, undersides, chest, and muzzle. Less white than this must be penalized proportionately. An inverted V blaze on the face is desirable. The Van bi-color must be white with color confined to the head, tail, and legs. One or two small, colored body patches are allowed.

The calico, a description used only in the United States, is a white cat with unbrindled patches of black and red. As a preferred minimum, the cat should have white feet, legs, undersides, chest, and muzzle. Any less white coloring than this will be penalized proportionately. An inverted V blaze on the face is desirable. The eye color must be brilliant copper.

The dilute-calico (including the Vans) is a white cat with

unbrindled patches of blue and cream. As a preferred minimum, the cat should have white feet, legs, undersides, chest, and muzzle. Any less white coloring than this will be penalized proportionately. An inverted V blaze on the face is desirable; the eye color must be brilliant copper.

The bi-color, including the Van bi-color, has a two-toned coat which may be black and white, blue and white, red and white, cream and white (only in the United States), or smoke and white. As a preferred minimum, the cat should have white feet, legs, undersides, chest, and muzzle; any less white coloring will be penalized proportionately. For the smoke-and-white, the colored areas of the coat must conform to the cur-rently-established smoke color Standards. An inverted V blaze on the face is desirable and the eye color must be a brilliant copper. In the United Kingdom, not less than one-third, and not more than half the coat must be white. The GCCF recognizes bi-colors in white and all the recognized solid colors and white, and all the recognized tabby colors. All these color combinations are listed under the GCCF general heading of bi-color long-hairs.

The Van bi-color may be red and white, blue and white, cream and white or smoke and white (only in the United States) and in the United Kingdom, chocolate and white and lilac and white the solid colors and white, and lilac and white. These are white cats with the color confined to the head, tail, and legs. In the United Kingdom, there should be no color on the body or legs. For the smoke-and-white in the United States, the coat's colored areas must conform to the smoke color Standards. One or two small colored patches on the white body are allowable. In the United Kingdom, up to three small spots of color are allowed. The eye color must be brilliant copper. The GCCF recognizes Van tri-colors in white and the recognized tortoiseshell colors of tortie-and-white, blue-tortie-and-white, chocolate-tortie-and-white, and lilac-tortie-and white.

The Van-calico is white with unbrindled black and red patches confined to the head, tail, and legs. One or two small, colored patches on the body are allowable. The eye color must be brilliant copper.

The Van-dilute-calico is white with unbrindled patches of blue and cream confined to the head, tail and legs. One or two small, colored patches on the body are allowable. The eye color must be brilliant copper. In the United States, cats having more than two small body spots are con-sidered to be regular bi-color Persians.

The tabby-and-white is white with colored portions that must con-form to the accepted classic, mackerel, or patched-tabby color Standards. As a preferred minimum, the cat should have white feet, legs, undersides, chest, and muzzle. Less white than this minimum will be penalized pro-portionately. An inverted V blaze on the face is desirable. The eye color must conform to the established tabby pattern requirements. The GCCF recognizes bi-color tabby-and-white in all the tabby colorings.

The Van-tabby-and-white is white with color confined to the extremities: the head, tail, and legs. The colored portions must conform to the accepted classic, mackerel, or patched-tabby color Standards. One or two small colored patches on the body are allowable. The eye color must conform to the established tabby pattern requirements.

The peke-faced-red and peke-faced-red tabby cats should conform in color and general type to the Standard for the red and the red tabby cats. The placement of the ears, which should conform with the underlying bone structure of the head, differs greatly from that of the standard Persian. The nose should be short, depressed, and indented between the eyes. The muzzle should be wrinkled. The eyes should be large, round, and set wide apart. The horizontal break, located between the usual nose break and the top dome of the head, should run straight across the front of the head, creating half-moon boning above the eyes and an additional horizontal indentation in the center of the forehead. This bone structure should give the impression of a very round head with a strong chin. The eye color must be brilliant copper.

THE HIMALAYAN DIVISION

Pointed-pattern cats or colorpoints, as they are known in the United Kingdom, were first given official GCCF recognition in 1955, and are consistently successful, top prize winners around the world. After World War II, a chance mating between a Siamese and probably a Persian blue, produced a remarkably attractive new color. This kitten was acquired by Brian Stirling-Webb, owner of the Briarry Cattery in Richmond, England. He started the first planned breeding of colorpoints and was soon joined by Mrs. S.M. Manton, who showed cats under her married name, Harding. Three years later the development of the American Himalayans was started by the late Mrs. Goforth.

When these breeders produced this lovely pointed pattern, they were producing what was to become one of the most popular Persians of all time. The name Himalayan, refers to the coat pattern common to the Himalayan rabbit. With the dark coloration of the ears, mask, legs, and tail contrasted with the lighter body color, set off by the sapphire-blue eyes, these Persians have catapulted in popularity.

For many years, the Himalayan was considered a hybrid of the Siamese and Persian. The fact that every desired feature was controlled by a recessive gene only heightened the challenge to breeders and geneticists. The CFA has only in the past few years made the Himalayan a Persian color and the accepted variations of coat color are many. In all cases the eye color must be a deep, vivid, sapphire-blue.

The groupings and descriptions for Himalayans differ slightly from country to country. This lovely color is usually known as colorpoint in most countries except the United States. In the United Kingdom they are arranged in four main groups: the solid colors with all the possible dilutes, then the tortie-point group, the tabby-points, and tortie-tabby-points.

The color range is extensive embracing the twenty colors genetically possible. The solid group consists of seal, blue, chocolate, lilac, red, and cream. The tortie colors are seal-tortie, blue-cream, chocolate-tortie, and lilac-cream. The tabby-points have five colors: seal-tabby, blue-tabby, chocolate-tabby, lilac-tabby, red-tabby, and cream-tabby. The tortie-tabby mixture of color and patterning has just four colors: seal-tortie-tabby, blue-cream-tabby, chocolate-tortie-tabby, and lilac-cream-tabby.

The seal-point's color is an even, pale, fawn to cream. It must be warm in tone, shading gradually into lighter color on the stomach and chest. The GCCF requires the body color to be creamy white, thus giving as much contrast as possible between body color and points. The points must be deep, seal-brown. The nose leather and paw pads must be the same color as the points.

The chocolate-point coat is ivory with no shading. The points are a milk-chocolate color and warm in tone. The nose leather and paw pads must be cinnamon-pink.

The lilac-point has glacial white coat color with no shading. The points must be a frosty gray with a pinkish tone. The nose leather and paw pads must be lavender pink. The GCCF describes the body color as magnolia-white.

The blue-point coat is bluish-white, cold in tone, shading gradually to white on the stomach and chest. The points must be blue and the nose leather and paw pads must be slate blue.

The flame- or red-point coat is creamy-white. The points must be deep orange-flame to deep red. The nose leather and paw pads must be flesh-colored or coral pink. The GCCF describes the body color as apricot-white.

The cream-point is creamy-white with no shading; the points must be buff-cream with no apricot. The nose leather and paw pads must be flesh pink or salmon-coral in color.

The seal-tortie-point has creamy white or pale fawn coat color. The points must be seal with unbrindled patches of red and/or cream. A blaze of red or cream on the face is desirable whereas the GCCF says that a facial blaze is permissible. The nose leather and paw pads must be seal-brown with flesh-and/or coral-pink mottling to conform with the colors of the points.

The blue-cream-point, called the blue tortie by some American associations, is bluish-white or creamy-white, shading gradually to white on the stomach and chest. The points must be blue with patches of cream. In the United Kingdom, the point color should be intermingled rather than patched. The nose leather and paw pads must be slate-blue, pink, or a combination of slate-blue-and-pink.

The lynx-point color class is for the seal-lynx-point, blue-lynx-point, tortie-lynx-point, blue-cream-lynx-point, flame-lynx-point, and cream-lynx-point all of which compete in the same color class. The seal-lynx-point, called the seal-tabby-point by the GCCF and FIFe, has points of beige-brown ticked with darker brown tabby markings. It must be pale cream to fawn and warm in tone. The mask must be clearly lined with dark stripes, vertical on the forehead. The forehead must have a classic M. Horizontal stripes on the cheeks, and dark spots on the whisker pads, clearly outlined in dark-colored edges are also a requirement. The inner ear must be light with a thumbprint on the outer ear. The markings must be dense, clearly defined, and broad. The legs must be evenly barred with bracelets. The tail must be barred, and there should not be striping or mottling on the body. Consideration is given to shading on older cats. The nose leather must be seal or brick-red and the paw pads must be seal.

The blue-lynx-point (known as the blue-tabby point by the GCCF and FIFe) has points which are light, silvery-blue, ticked with darker blue tabby markings. The body color is bluish-white and cold in tone. The mask must be clearly lined with dark stripes, vertical on the forehead, and a classic M must appear on the forehead. This color must have horizontal stripes on the cheeks and dark spots on whisker pads clearly outlined. The inner ear must be light with a thumbprint on the outer ear. The markings must be dense, clearly-defined, and broad. The legs must be evenly barred with bracelets. The tail must be barred and there should be no striping or mottling on the body. Consideration is given for shading in older cats. The nose leather must be blue or brick-red and the paw pads blue. The GCCF and FIFe also recognize chocolate-tabby-points where the points appear on a light bronze background with ivory-white body color and lilac-tabby-points with lilac markings on a pale beige background and magnolia-white body color.

The seal-tortie lynx point which the GCCF describes as the seal-tortie-tabby point has beige-brown points with dark brown tabby markings, and patches of red. The body color is either cream-white or pale fawn. The mask must be clearly lined with dark, vertical, stripes and a classic M on the forehead. Horizontal stripes on the cheeks are required as are dark spots on the clearly outlined whisker pads. The inner ear must be light with a thumbprint on the outer ear. The markings must be dense, clearly-defined, and broad, and the tail and legs must be evenly-barred with bracelets. The nose leather and paw pads must be seal-brown and/or flesh- or coral-pink.

The blue-cream-lynx-point, called blue-tortie-lynx in some associations, has blue points, with darker blue, tabby markings, and patches of cream. The GCCF describes this color as blue-cream-tabby-point. The body color is bluish-white and cold in tone. The mask must be clearly lined; the forehead must have dark, vertical stripes and a classic M. Horizontal stripes must appear on the cheeks. Dark spots on the whisker pads must be clearly outlined. The inner ear must be light with a thumbprint on the outer ear. The markings must be dense, clearly-defined and broad; the legs and tail must be evenly barred with bracelets. The nose leather and paw pads must be slate-blue and/or pink.

The flame-or red-lynx point (known as the red-tabby-point by the GCCF and FIFe) has points which are deep, orange-flame-ticked with deep red, tabby markings; the body color is creamy-white. The mask must be clearly lined; with dark stripes vertical on the forehead as well as a classic M; horizontal stripes on the cheeks; and dark clearly outlined spots on the whisker pads. The inner ear must be light with a thumbprint on the outer ear. The markings must be dense, clearly-defined, and broad; the legs must be evenly barred with bracelets. The tail must be barred, and there should be no striping or mottling on the body. Shading in older cats is allowed. The nose leather and paw pads must be flesh or coral-pink.

The cream-lynx-point (in the GCCF and FIFe referred to as the cream-tabby-point) has pale, cream-ticked points with dark, creamy tabby markings; the body is creamy-white. The mask must be clearly lined with dark stripes; vertical stripes and a classic M on the forehead; horizontal stripes on the cheeks; and dark clearly outlined spots on the whisker pads. The inner ear must be light with a thumbprint on the outer ear. The markings must be dense, clearly defined, and broad. The legs must be evenly barred with bracelets, and the tail must also be barred. The nose leather and paw pads must be flesh or coral-pink in color. GCCF and FIFe also recognize chocolate- and lilac-tabby point colorpoints.

The other pointed color class is for the chocolate-tortie-points and the lilac-cream points that compete in the same color class. The chocolate-tortie-point is ivory with no shading; the points, chocolate with unbrindled patches of red and/or cream. The nose leather and paw pads must be chocolate with flesh- and/or coral-pink mottling to conform with the point color. The eye color must be deep, vivid blue. The lilac-cream point is glacial-white with no shading; the points are lilac with patches of cream. The nose leather and paw pads must be lavender-pink, pink, or a combination of lavender-pink and pink. The eye color must be deep, vivid blue. There are additional colors recognized by other cat associations, however, those mentioned here account for about ninety-nine percent of the Persians seen in the show ring throughout the world.

Ch. Kewlocke, a black smoke, was the winner of over sixty first and special prizes, including Best American Bred Cat on two occasions. He is pictured here in 1909.

CHAPTER VIII

A GALLERY OF BEAUTIFUL PERSIANS

The cat Fancy has provided a showcase for breakthroughs in breeding through the years, and has demonstrated the direction breeders must take to produce beautiful and healthy cats. Prize-winning cats have influenced the direction of the Fancy by moving a step closer to realizing

White Aigrette, a blue-eyed white, was considered in 1909 to be one of the most perfect white queens that could be shown. Her record of prizes included firsts in 1908 in Boston and Chicago, and Best Cat in Show in Hartford, Connecticut in 1909.

perfection and providing a means of improving the gene pool. Many examples of extraordinary Persians have appeared on the show bench and therefore it is particularly difficult to provide a summary of superstars, since there have been so many.

The serious breeding of Persians began in the United Kingdom and the United States at the turn of the century when the first stud books were compiled. These contained details of pedigrees and registered birth

This black Persian, Cyrus the Great, was the foundation male for the Cyrus Persian Cattery in Garden City, Kansas and the winner of many top awards in the early 1900s. Although his ears are large and pointed, he appears to have deep eye color, an asset on today's show bench.

Ch. Petie K had the distinction of being the only American bred cream champion shown at the time. His prizes included firsts in New York in each year from 1906-1908.

A great show cat in his time, Ch. Lord Kew Tangerine, an orange Persian, would be judged in the solid color class today as a red, where his obvious tabby markings, large ears, and lack of type would all be faulted. Lord Kew won top show awards in 1907 and 1908.

Ch. Rob Roy II of Arrandale, a Chinchilla imported to America from England at great expense, was the only Chinchilla male champion in England at the time. He took top prizes in Birmingham in 1907, at the Botanic Gardens and Crystal Palace shows in London in 1908, and Steyning in 1908.

Ch. Argent Splendor, a Chinchilla silver, was the first of his color to become a champion in America. Owned by Mrs. Champion, a prominant name in both the American and English cat Fancy, this cat won many prizes including Best Cat in Show in New York and Chicago in 1905. Today judges would find fault with his lack of a strong chin.

Ch. Birkdale Ruffie, a famous brown tabby, bred in England by Miss Southam, scored his first success in 1894. At the 1896 Crystal Palace Show he swept the board winning five prizes including the special prize given by the Prince of Wales, who was soon to become king. Because of his expression and rich sable color, he was often the model for the famous illustrator, Louis Wain.

information. Very few photographs or other detailed information about the appearance of cats from this period survive, except for publications such as *The Book of the Cat* by Frances Simpson, published by Cassell & Company, in 1903. Apart from the stud books, records of this period are sketchy until just after World War II.

PRE-WORLD WAR II

Evelyn Langston began breeding her famous blues and Chinchillas in the United Kingdom just after World War I and continued her work for fifty years. The names of her cats were followed by her affix "of Allington." In her professional life she taught singing at the Royal Academy of Music in London, but she obviously spent a great deal of time breeding and showing her Persians, for her influence on the breed was profound. In GCCF stud book number three covering the period of 1923-27, no fewer than ten Chinchillas owned or bred by Evelyn Langston are listed. One of her famous stud cats was Duffy of Allington and nearly all English Chinchillas have this famous male somewhere in their pedigrees.

Ch. Vera of Allington's robust physique and beauty led to this cat, bred by Evelyn Langston, winning seven championships.

Some of her other notable stud cats were Ch. Rodney of Allington and Ch. Flambeau of Allington. She also owned Ch. Foxburrow Tilli Willi bred by P.M. Soderberg. The Allington cats were noted for their overall beauty and robust physiques.

In the late 1940s Molly Turney became fascinated by the beauty of the Chinchilla. Books from this period often refer to a Chinchilla as "the fairy princesses" of the cat world. Turney registered the prefix "Bonavia" in England and began one of the most prolific Chinchilla breeding lines.

Molly Turney exhibited Ch. Arisbury Aphra in 1952. The cat won many prizes in England.

Ch. Jemari Justine, bred by Rosemary Gowdy, sired many prize-winning cats found all over the world.

She concluded after some years that the Chinchilla gene pool was very limited and that constant inbreeding was proving detrimental to the vigor and robustness of her Persians, resulting in a number of kittens with fragile bone structures. To remedy this, she imported three Chinchillas to England from the United States, none of which was suitable for the English show bench. However, these cats brought in fresh bloodlines which helped Turney to breed strong, healthy kittens. The Bonavia line was best known for its deep, rich, green eye color and robustness. The progeny of the Bonavias is scattered widely throughout the world and few Chinchilla pedigrees fail to show this prefix in their backgrounds.

One of the longest established breeders of Chinchillas in the United Kingdom is Rosemary Gowdy whose prefix is "Jemari." Her basic stock came from the Bonavia lines and she has built on that success. The Jemari Chinchillas are noted for their excellent type and temperament. Gowdy's outstanding male, Ch. Jemari Justine, was born in 1973, lived for twelve years, and sired many prize-winning cats. He became Best Longhair Adult in Show on five occasions and one of his sons, Maximilian, was exported to Germany, and gained the title of Grand

International Champion at the early age of eleven and one-half months. Offspring of the Jemaris are found in fourteen countries where they win the highest awards.

SOLID COLORS

The basis for many of the colors in the Persian range comes from the solid color cats. Dorrie Brice-Webb, one of England's longest-serving judges, acquired her first blue in 1933. In 1935 her husband gave her another, Bonne Yvonne, as a wedding present. From her second blue using the prefix "Ronada" Brice-Webb bred one of the best-known and most prolific studs in the period before World War II, King Kong. She was one of a small band of breeders who managed to struggle through the difficult rationing period of the war, when food was in short supply for humans with little to spare for pets. From 1948 until the early 1990s she judged shows in the United Kingdom and other countries and in 1982 she

Dorrie Brice-Webb's most famous blue was the prize-winning King Kong, rated one of the best blues in England in the late 1940s.

was honored by FIFe with the title, Honorary Judge, one of only two judges to ever be awarded this title in the United Kingdom.

Joan Thompson began breeding Persians in the United Kingdom in the early 1950s, using the affix "of Pensford." She became a very dis-

Ch. Octavian of Pensford, bred by Joan Thompson, was awarded seventy-five firsts in the mid-1950s at English shows. Octavian was a beautiful blue remembered for his wonderful temperament.

tinguished and long-serving judge of the Persian breed. Her outstanding males included Ch. Octavian of Pensford who was the winner of many first prizes and Best in Show awards. Among his progeny was a beautiful cream female exported to the United States, Triple Ch. Lady Gay of Pensford. Many of Thompson's cream, blue, and blue-cream kittens were exported around the world, and became international champions in Switzerland, Denmark, and other countries. The Pensford cats were noted for their strong, powerful physiques and wonderful temperaments.

At about the same time another distinguished judge and breeder of blues became well established in England. Marguerite Brunton had the affix "of Dunesk" and bred gorgeous blues. Her affix appears in the background of many of today's cats. Her outstanding contribution was to establish a soft, pale, pastel color.

This prize-winning blue, Dazzler of Dunesk, bred by Marguerite Brunton, won a string of first prizes and was subsequently exported to New Zealand.

Ch. Gaydene Genevieve, shown with her breeder, Lily McVady, was winner of the Blue Persian Championship shows in 1955, 1957, and 1958.

The other outstanding English breeder/judge of this period was Lily McVady who bred blues, creams, and blue-creams from 1950-80. Ch. Gaydene Rudolph was Best Exhibit at the Blue Persian Cat Show in 1952. Another of her cats, Ch. Gaydene Genevieve, was triple winner of the Blue Persian Championship shows of 1955, 1957, and 1958. The progeny of these lovely "Gaydene" Persians did much to improve general standards of health, physique, and type.

The Shawnee line of Persians in the United States, owned by Nikki Horner, produced the copper-eyed white male, Gr. Ch. Shawnee

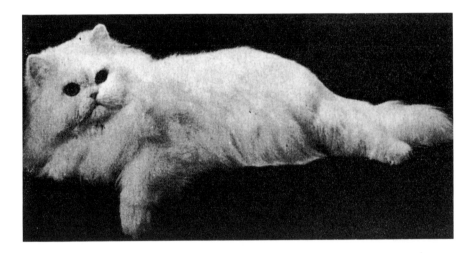

Gr. Ch. Shawnee Moonflight, bred by Nikki Horner, became a grand champion in 1960 and then won three Cat of the Year awards, a record that has never been beaten in the United States.

Moonflight. This cat became a grand champion in 1960 and went on to be the Cat of the Year three times, a record that has never been beaten. Horner's Persians continued to inspire other breeders, taking top prizes in virtually every show in which they were exhibited. Other memorable Shawnee grand champions were Shawnee Antiseptic, a copper-eyed white; and Paintin' the Town Red II, a self-red.

An English breeder/judge with a dazzling run of success is Jean Hogan with her "Snowhite" Persians. She started breeding in 1960, when she purchased a blue from Peggy Denton called Camber Suzanne, who soon became a champion. Mated to a popular stud, Ch. Snowcloud Crispin, she produced an outstanding kitten named Giselle. Giselle won best in show honors each time shown. Hogan also bred Ch. Showhite Herald, the only cat to have won the Best in Show title at the National Cat Club Show in London in four consecutive years. This cat was one of the most glamorous white Persians possible to imagine, with a wonderfully strong, well-boned physique, and a long, flowing coat always groomed to perfection. Jean Hogan bred many other famous Persians including Champions Snowhite Jewel, Brigitte, Heraldson, Enchantment, Sylphide, and Elegance. There are international champions of her breeding in Belgium and Switzerland. During her active showing career Jean Hogan won a staggering forty-two Best in Show awards.

Some of the best cream Persians shown in the United Kingdom for several decades were those bred by Marlene Howes under her prefix "Honeymist." They were of outstanding quality and of the very palest, milky-cream color. These creams were highly sought after, have become champions, and have won the highest awards in countries around the world. She has produced dozens of champions in cream, blue-cream, white, black, blue, tortie, and red.

Gr. Ch. Foxavon Alaskan Superior, bred by Audrey Newsome, was only one of the many spectacular whites she bred.

Audrey Newsome, of the Foxavon prefix, has bred some notable blues and whites. She visited the Simbelair cattery, owned by Lois Weston in Canada, and upon her return to the United Kingdom imported Simbelair Mapleleaf Sioux, the foundation of her very successful stock. She bred Gr. Ch. Foxavon Sharon, a beautiful blue; Ch. Foxavon Marina, an orange-eyed white; and Ch. Foxavon Teromaa, an odd-eyed white in addition to many other champions. Gr. Ch. Foxavon Alaskan Superior was one of her most spectacular cats.

Among successful breeders of modern-type, solid colors in the United Kingdom is Isobella Bangs, who works under the prefix "Lafrabella." She regularly produces kittens of the quality which are

Gr. Ch. Lafrabella Oh Lala, bred by Isobella Bangs, won top prizes in England in 1988 and 1989. This odd-eyed white shows many of the qualities which are sought by Persian breeders throughout the world.

sought after by those who wish to breed this Persian type. She also breeds Persians of traditional type. Her kittens have been sent to many countries around the world, including Malaysia. One of her outstanding whites was Ch. Lafrabella Oh Lala, which gained the award of Best in Show at the White Persian Cat Club Show and the Capital Longhaired Cat Show in 1988 and 1989.

SILVA-WYTE and JB CATTERIES

In Memoriam

Gr. Ch. Silva-Wyte Jack-A-Napes of JB

May 27, 1964 - November 7, 1970

By Gr. Ch. Vel-Vene VooDoo of Silva-Wyte

x Silva-Wyte Tiffany

Gr. Ch. Silva-Wyte Trafari of JB

From cat of the year to

Mother of the year.

Gr. Ch. Silva-Wyte Elmer Fudd
(son of Jackie)

Gr. Ch. JB Moor of Silva-Wyte
Son of Trafari

RICHARD H. GEBHARDT
SILVA-WYTE

JOHN BANNON
JB CATTERY

77 Diamond Spring Rd.
Denville, N. J. 07834
201-627-3108
Registered with CFA only

A 1971 ad for the Silva-Wyte Cattery gives a sampling of the quality blacks Richard Gebhardt produced over the years.

Greg and Judy Brocato have consistently bred outstanding Persians including solid color Persians year after year. They run one of the most outstanding American catteries in Rome, Georgia, Southpaw Cattery. In the last twenty years they have had twenty-one National Winners and an additional three with cats they owned and exhibited. The Southpaw cats are known for their beautiful coats and eye color. In 1993 the Brocato's copper-eyed white took the top award in the United States, Cat of the Year. The Brocato cats have also won top prizes in Europe and Japan.

Gr. Ch. Vel-Vene Voo Doo of Silva-Wyte, owned by Richard Gebhardt of the Silva-Wyte Cattery in the United States, was one of the most memorable black Persians, putting his stamp on the look of all blacks to follow. Voo Doo was the descendent of two great Persians: Gr. Ch. Lavender Liberty Beau (Sire) and Gr. Ch. Pied Piper of Barbe Bleue (great grand sire). Voo Doo was Cat of the Year in 1959 and sire to many other great Persians including Gr. Ch. Silva-Wyte Trafari of J.B., the 1966-67 Cat of the Year.

Some of the best black Persians in the United Kingdom were bred by Marjorie Bull, who started her lines with a cat named Vigilant Mark, the son of Marguerite Brunton's Jewel of Dunesk. Under her prefix "Deebank", Bull bred some of the best black Persians seen on the show bench during the last few decades.

SHADED COLORS

Gwen Webb's Silver Mesa silvers were at their best in the late

Ch. Sir Ronlore of Silver Mesa is one of the Chinchillas of quality Gwen Webb bred in the late 1950s and early 1960s.

Julio, one of the prize-winning Walnut Hill silvers, which Dory Weston produced in California in the late 1960s.

1950s and early 1960s and pointed the way, in terms of quality, for all silver breeders to follow. Following World War II, she imported Francis of Allington from England and exported Silver Mesa Apache to England. Webb's cats have contributed strong bone structure and beautiful coat quality to this color. Grace Over's Gray Ivy silvers were the big prize winners from 1967-72 in the United States. Her silvers won countless Best in Show awards. At the same time, great silvers were being produced by Dory Weston of Walnut Hill cattery, Irene Buchan of Wee Heather cattery, and by many members of the California Silver Fanciers. In Pasadena, California, in November 1964, the California Silver Fanciers held their first Silver Showcase show, managed by Will Thompson with more than 100 silvers in competition. Several years after this first show, the Silver Showcast show registered twenty-six grand champions for competition.

SMOKES

Many breeders have contributed to the quality of smokes of all colors seen on today's show benches. A detailed list would be lengthy indeed. One of those who contributed a great deal to the quality is the judge, Doreen Hoyle whose "Hardendale" prefix appears in the pedigrees of innumerable smokes and cameos. She achieved her first success in the 1960s with Ch. Hardendale Nicholas, the son of the famous stud cat, Ch. Orion of Pensford. Nicholas retired unbeaten in Open classes after over thirty appearances and after being awarded twenty-two challenge certificates. His offspring are scattered around the world and his name appears in many of the smoke and associated color pedigrees. Hoyle later became very interested in the cameo when they were first developed and she bred the United Kingdom's first shaded-cameo, grand premier, Hardendale Carrioca; followed by the first red-shaded female champion, Hardendale Enchantress; and the first cream-shaded female champion, Hardendale Eugenie. She has bred scores of champions in the United Kingdom and many champions, grand champions, and international champions from the Hardendale lines are found in other countries.

Joan O'Hara, who owns the Araho Cattery in New Jersey produced great black smokes that took top honors in the United States in 1967-71. She also bred outstanding blacks, winning kitten of the year in 1971 with her female, Gr. Ch. Fanci-Pantz Petti Girl of Araho, which went on to become Cat of the Year in 1979. O'Hara continues to show and win top prizes for her Persians.

Patricia Lichtenberg runs the Palmetto Cattery in the United States and breeds beautiful black smokes and tortie smokes. Winners of many Best in Show awards, these cats are known not only for their excellent type, but also for their beautiful color. Many of the Palmetto cats have been exported to Europe where they win top prizes.

TABBIES

Brown tabbies are a challenge to breeders. It is very difficult to combine excellent type and correct tabby markings. Betty Conway started with brown tabbies in 1977 in the United Kingdom and bred champions, international and grand international champions. Her cats have done much to improve the general qualities in this lovely, old breed, under her prefix "Kaiwan."

Mr. and Mrs. George Saunders have also achieved success with brown tabbies and bi-colors under the prefix "Chermician." One of their outstanding cats is a red-and-white bi-color, named Gr. Ch. Chermician Santa Fe. Helen and Leonard Smith's Smithway Cattery in San Diego, California, produced and exhibited some great red tabbies, including one

Joan O'Hara's Gr. Ch. Fanci-Pantz Petti Girl of Araho became Cat of the Year in 1979 in the United States.

of their foundation cats, Gr. Ch. Spero Stink Puff of Smithway. They went on to produce peke-faced red tabbies in the 1960s, still considered the best of that variety.

PARTI-COLORS

Until Norah Woodifield took an interest in selective breeding of tortie-and-whites and bi-color Persians, these lovely colors had not made a great deal of progress in the United Kingdom. She started breeding under her prefix "Pathfinders" in 1930. One of her most beautiful cats was Ch. Pathfinders May Flower, who won ten Challenge Certificates between 1961 and 1965 and was twice Best Persian Cat in Show. In all, Norah Woodifield bred sixty-five champions. She also became a cat judge, like so many other English breeders, and there was never any problem in finding her at shows, for her bright pink hair was quite distinctive.

Bill and Gayle Lee's Cat of the Year in 1980-81, Gr. Ch. Lee's Let the Sunshine In, was a cream-and-white bi-color male which set a precedent in style, setting this cat apart from many others. The Lees have worked hard to develop and perfect bi-colors and calicos and have led the way for other breeders of these colors.

The cats bred and shown by Jim Rambo of Atlanta, Georgia, have made their mark in the show world. In particular, Gr. Ch. Rambo's Rocky Mountain Sunrise, a red-and-white bi-color male, was an excellent example of the modern type. Rocky was Cat of the Year in 1986 and had a friendly, affectionate temperament. The Rambo bloodlines produced another top winner in 1989-90, Gr. Ch. Jarien's Southern Belle of Rambo, a calico that was Second Best Kitten that season.

Anne Waddington who owns the ANZ cattery in Mechanicsburg, Pennsylvania, has produced excellent bi-colors and calicos through the years. Her Gr. Ch. ANZ Jeepers Creepers, a dilute calico female, was fourth best kitten and second best Cat of the Year in 1988-89. In 1989-90 Gr. Ch. ANZ Betty Boop of Pajean, a black-and-white bi-color female was Fourth Best Kitten and in 1993 her dilute calico female, Ch. ANZ Toy, was winner in both the kitten and adult categories.

Barbara Patch has specialized in tortoiseshells and other associated colors, under the prefix "Honeycharm." One of the most beautiful cats seen on the shown bench was Supreme Gr. Ch. Honeycharm Jasmine, glowing with rich color and of wonderful Persian type. This cat was always highly admired and still retains her beauty now that she is quite advanced in years. In 1985 she won the title of Supreme Best Overall Cat at the Supreme Show in the United Kingdom. Jasmine is one of the most gentle and affectionate cats a judge can handle.

Barbara Patch's Supreme Gr. Ch. Honeycharm
Jasmine, seen here with her breeder/owner, won
fourteen grand challenge certificates in a row.

COLORPOINTS

There have been many successful breeders of one of the most striking of Persian colors, the colorpoints. No list of breeders would be of any value without mentioning the enormous contribution to their progress made by Mrs. Harding. She was a zoologist and had vast knowledge of genetics. Under her prefix "Mingchiu," she consistently bred colorpoints of beauty, elegance, and quality. Ch. Mingchiu Mandarin of Sahadi at only one year of age won thirty-four English awards and was the first colorpoint to become an international champion in the United Kingdom *and* the United States in 1965. Ch. Mingchiu Chou-Lu won Best Kitten in Show twice, and later became Best Colorpoint Adult at the National Cat Club Show in 1967. He had a fantastic coat, reaching five and one-half inches in length; a wide, round head; and a short nose. He had well-set ears and a wide top of head. His body was compact and low to the ground. His very pale coat contrasted strikingly with his seal points. The first chocolate-point colorpoint in the United Kingdom was Ch. Minchiu Ptan in 1968, followed by the first lilac-point colorpoint, Ch. Mingchiu Sulafour in 1969.

Anne and Ben Borret bred the very first Himalayans of note in Calgary, Canada. They used the bloodlines of Brian Stirling-Webb to pro-

Will Thompson's Gr. Ch. Chestermere Chahila, bred by the Borrets of Calgary, Canada, was the first top-winning Himalayan in the United States.

Another top prize-winning Himalayan was Gr. Ch. Quicksilver's Cascade, bred by Will Thompson.

duce some of the finest Himalayans to appear on the American show bench. Their cats set the tone for this variety when Anne Borret began to show Chestermere Chen Soo in the United States. The Borret's Gr. Ch. Chestermere Kinuba, owned by judge Boris Teron and Larry Keely, served as a great sire. The Borret's Gr. Ch. Chestermere Chahila, owned by Will Thompson, was the first top-winning Himalayan, taking top prizes in 1969 and 1970 and was chosen Best Cat in Show a record forty-one times. Chahila's daughter, Gr. Ch. Quiksilver's Cascade was chosen as Best Himalayan in the United States in 1971. The Chestermere Himalayans dominated the American show bench from 1965 through 1971.

Several colorpoint breeders are currently continuing the improvement in type and quality, and to list them all is quite impossible. Anne Bailey has bred some of the most glamorous colorpoints seen in the United Kingdom and presently the Baileys have sixteen Grand Champions they have bred living with them. One of the most beautiful is United Kingdom Gr. Ch. Anneby Scallywag. This magnificent blue colorpoint was never beaten on the show bench. When he gained the splendid title he now holds, he was retired unbeaten. Other outstanding cats produced by the Baileys are Gr. Ch. Ragamuffin, another blue colorpoint. Gr. Ch. Anneby Iddy Biddy, a female seal colorpoint; Gr. Ch. Anneby Charisma, a lilac-cream colorpoint female; and Gr. Ch. Anneby Enchantress, a blue-cream colorpoint. Under her prefix of "Anneby" she has produced grand champions in many of the other colorpoint colors including cream and lilacs.

PERSIANS OF MANY COLORS

Joyce and Bob Worth, both cat judges, are particularly well known for their beautiful Birmans, but they have regarded the breeding of

International Premier Rojodanco Diodante, a blue Persian bred by Joyce and Bob Worth, won many top honors in England and was finally exported to Germany.

Persians in a wide range of colors as something of a challenge. In responding to this challenge they have made a positive contribution to the quality of Persians in the United Kingdom in the blue, cream, blue-cream, tortie, red, and black colors. Among their outstanding cats are International Premier Rojodanco Diodante, a blue Persian living in Germany and International Ch. Rojodanco Mrs. Whiskers, a black smoke living in Sweden where she gained her title in 1992. She was given this name as a kitten because she had the longest whiskers the breeders had ever seen. Another superb cat was the Worths' International European Ch. Rojodanco Prunella, a blue-cream. Rojodanco Star Trek, a blue, became

Cat of the Year in Australia.

Michael and Brenda Barrett became interested in Persians in 1965 and bought Wistaria of Dunesk from Marguerite Brunton. From this cat they bred Ch. Finchfield Showpiece, a blue-cream, and two international champion creams. They continue to breed blues, whites, and blue-creams with ever-growing success. Finchfield Michael became a champion at age fifteen months and eventually became the United Kingdom's first long-haired grand champion, retiring unbeaten at twenty months of age. The superb quality of their stock in a wide range of colors, has been seen in many countries around the world.

CHAPTER IX

THE PERSIAN AROUND THE WORLD

The cat Fancy is alive and well in many countries. Every weekend, at least one cat show or exhibition is held somewhere in the world and at each show, there will be examples of the Persian. The breed quite often will represent the largest number of cats entered. The largest proportion of pedigreed cats registered in the world are, in fact, Persians.

Generally there are differences in the rules and Standards of each cat association, but in the case of the Persian, the Standard is very similar internationally. The controversy over the modern-types versus traditional-types is the only major difference in the Persian Standard and its interpretation worldwide. The cats which are considered to be the most desirable by the general public will prevail, no matter what each Standard dictates.

THE EUROPEAN CONNECTION

In Europe, the largest sanctioning body is FIFe, the Feline International Federation. Each member country registers its cats according to rules agreed with FIFe, but uses the same Standards and judge-training program as FIFe. There are other cat associations in Europe, but most of these work with a Persian Standard that is very similar to FIFe's. The member-countries in FIFe, including some not located in Europe, are Argentina, Austria, Belgium, Brazil, the Czech Republic, Denmark, Finland, France, Germany, Hungary, Italy, Liechtenstein, Luxembourg, Malaysia, Mexico, Norway, the Netherlands, Poland, Portugal, San Marino, Spain, Sweden, Switzerland, Slovakia, Slovenia, and the United Kingdom. Probationary members are Australia, Belorussia, Croatia, Estonia, Iceland, Israel, Latvia, Lithuania, and the Ukraine.

Although this may appear an impressive list of FIFe members, the actual number of cats and members—considering the frequency and num-

Eric Wickham-Ruffle judging Persians in Moscow. There is a fast developing cat Fancy in eastern Europe, notably in countries which used to belong to the former Soviet Union.

ber of shows—is far greater within the independent cat associations in Europe. Many of these have joined forces, working in unison. There is also a movement to unify the registration procedures for all European cat associations under European Community regulations.

A good way to understand the basics about any cat association is to determine what is not allowed for any breed or color. The FIFe Persian Standard includes a longer list of faults and details for disqualification or withholding awards than the American or British Standard. A review shows that FIFe strongly discourages the proliferation of genetic defects and any improper treatment of the animals, basic rules which hold true for all international cat associations. There is a difference in the allocation of points between the CFA Persian Standard and FIFe's, as can be seen by comparing the CFA point scale on page 143 with FIFe's below.

TYPE (including shape, size, bone structure, length of
tail, height, and thickness of leg):   20 points

HEAD (including general head shape, shape and set of eyes,
ear shape and set, nose length and width, stop,
jaw, forehead, teeth):   30 points

COLOR (eye color):   15 points

COAT (including color, texture, quality, tabby
markings, points, even patching, etc.):   30 points

CONDITION (grooming and preparation, presentation):   5 points

TOTAL: 100 points

The FIFe Persian Standard is very precise in its descriptions of the Persian colors for it gives details of the subtle color changes of the coat as the cat matures. CFA's color descriptions are less detailed requiring a judge to have a great deal of knowledge of the nuances of color in the developmental stages. FIFe's Standard contains special remarks to assist a judge when assessing color, very helpful for visiting judges less familiar with the FIFe Standard.

FIFe recognizes some Persian colors and patterns not recognized by some American associations. Among these are the lilac-smoke, chocolate-silver tabby, chocolate tabby, mackerel-lilac-silver tabby, mackerel-lilac-tortie-silver tabby, and many colors of spotted tabby Persians, including, for example, the spotted-black-golden tabby, blue Chinchilla, blue-shaded-silver, chocolate-shaded-silver, lilac-shaded-silver, and the lilac-tortoiseshell-harlequin. These colors are quite rare and seldom, if ever, seen on the American show bench. In the United States the harlequin is identified as the Van-calico.

THE NEW ZEALAND CAT FANCY

Perhaps the most complex set of Standards today have been drawn up by the New Zealand Fancy. They have included a description of every possible color, and the long list is quite overwhelming. When Will Thompson was invited to judge in New Zealand, he questioned the length of this Standard and was told that he would not see many of these colors but the Standard was so comprehensive so as to properly assess any color which might appear for registration and judging. Because of its great length, the New Zealand Standard is printed as two separate books.

Some of the more unusual New Zealand Persians described in the Standard are the smoke-point and silver-point colorpoints (Himalayans). The New Zealand Standard requires that these cats have an undercoat that is silvery on the points. Once at a show in France a magnificent chocolate-smoke-point Himalayan Persian was entered, which proves that the unusual colors described by the New Zealand Fancy, do indeed exist. The difference as to what makes a cat a silver-point versus smoke-point is so minor, as to be relatively impossible to determine, unless the exhibit is a perfect example of the color. The silver-point tends to have a less silvery undercoat on the points than does the smoke-point, a very subtle difference.

In general the Persians in New Zealand are exquisite. The cameos in Dunedin are marvels to behold, with their very long coats, red-tipped color, and deep copper eyes. Shows in Auckland, Christchurch, Nelson, and Dunedin all have many excellent cats and kittens being exhibited.

AUSTRALIA

Australian cat shows are run in part according to GCCF protocol. Judges move from cage to cage evaluating the exhibits entered in multiple classes and general, open categories. The cats are also evaluated in special side classes such as best coat, best eye color, best tail, best body, etc. The sanctioning body for shows is different in each Australian state and often

Gold double Gr. Ch. Tuam New Sensation, a cream and white male, was bred by Kathie Scallan in Australia. Some Australian Fanciers are breeding modern-type Persians from American and English bloodlines.

there are several in one state—even as many as six.

Due in part to Australia's quarantine on imported cats, breeders have concentrated on perfecting the coat and eye color of their breeds. Australian Persians have luxurious coats which literally drag the floor when in full bloom. The colors are magnificent and approach perfection. The Chinchilla-silver, or "chinny" as the Australians call this color is very popular. Throughout Australia, large classes of Chinchillas are shown with beautiful tipping; long, flowing coats; and gorgeous green and blue-green eye color. In all classes examples of outstanding coat color and pattern are found. It is not uncommon to see blazing, copper eye color in the solid and other Persian colors in which this striking eye color is permitted.

In Tasmania, members of the cat Fancy are very dedicated and have invested much to improve the Persian breed. Many of Tasmania's Persians are of the modern-type. The Fanciers of Melbourne produce large, beautiful shows where the Chinchilla entry can be one hundred or more. Cheryl Uren, Dennis Turner, and Leonie Birch are all hard-working, experienced breeders of Persians. Cheryl Uren's whites and blues and Dennis Turner's calicos and colorpoints are noteworthy because coat colors are superb.

The Australian National Shows, held in different states of Australia annually attract sizable entries of all Persian colors. The best kitten, the best altered cat, and the best entire cat compete for the prestigious title of Supreme Exhibit at these shows.

THE JAPANESE CAT FANCY

The cat Fancy in Japan owes a great deal to Madame Shirane, who was instrumental in its founding, due to her great love of the Persian

Baron and Madame Shirane with their Persian kittens. Madame Shirane was the founder of the cat Fancy in Japan.

breed. Madame Shirane owned a cattery in Tokyo where she bred blue-eyed, white Persians. The cat Fancy in Japan has grown into a national effort to breed and exhibit beautiful cats. Most Japanese shows are held under the sponsorship of the many CFA clubs which breed their Persians using the American CFA Standard.

Cat shows in Tokyo and in Osaka and other Japanese cities are well managed and produced. In Osaka, the major organizer in the Fancy is Sumiko Akamatsu. Her Red Pine Cattery focuses on producing high-quality, bi-colors and calicos. Most cats exhibited at Japanese shows are

208

Will Thompson judging in Japan. Japanese cat shows are characterized by good organization and the majority of cats exhibited are Persians.

Persians: either whites or silvers. However, other colors, particularly black, are appearing. Outstanding copper-eyed whites, blacks, or silvers are often Best in Show. Many are imports from the United States but the Japanese are breeding many gorgeous Persians of their own. Silvers from Teruko Arai's cattery in Yokohama are appearing on the show benches in other countries.

Japan has many very knowledgeable cat Fanciers and beautiful exhibits. The variety of breeds at shows has increased, as has the proliferation of colors and patterns. Much of the progress is due to the help of Bess Higuchi, a translator for the United States Government in Japan, who has spent many hours escorting American judges in Japan, and easing their way by using her talents, charm, and her mastery of the languages and understanding of the cultures of both countries.

THE HAWAIIAN FANCY

Hawaii presents a particular challenge to the Persian breeder and owner. Fleas abound and fungus grows easily in this warm, tropical climate. Cat owners must be particularly attentive to flea control and signs of fungus. Hawaiian Persians are very beautiful, but tend to have less coat than those in colder climates. Hawaiian cat Fanciers love the extreme, modern-type cats; but must deal with problems presented in importing due to the quarantine restrictions to insure that rabies is not introduced to this paradise.

All cats imported to Hawaii must be placed in quarantine for three months. The quarantine station in Honolulu is a beautifully designed complex where each cat is provided with its own spacious compartment. The staff feeds and cares for the cats, but the importer is welcome to visit every day. The owner can also arrange a visit from the family vet.

Honolulu shows generally have more than 125 entries. With all the problems associated with maintaining a longhaired cat in a tropical climate, the Hawaiian Persians are particularly superb. Honolulu cat Fanciers spend great amounts of time and money assuring that their cats are of the finest quality.

CAT REGISTERIES AND ASSOCIATIONS

There are six cat registeries in North America. Each one is an independent association, with its own registration and show rules, breed Standards, publication, and year-end award winners. Owners of Persian cats who would like to join a Persian specialty or all-breed club should contact their registry at the addresses listed below and ask for details of such clubs in the area.

North America Cat Associations :

ACA,   The American Cat Association, Office of the Secretary, 8101 Katherine Ave., Panorama City, CA 91402

ACFA,   The American Cat Fanciers' Assciation, Office of the Secretary, P.O. Box 208, Point Lookout, MO 65726

CCA,   The Canadian Cat Association, Office of the Secretary, 88 Kennedy Road South, Unit 1805, Crampton, Ontario, Canada L6W 3PS

CFA,   The Cat Fanciers' Association, Inc., CFA Central Office, P.O. Box 1005, Manasquan, NJ 08736-0805

CFF,   The Cat Fanciers' Federation, Office of the Secretary, 9509 Montgomery Road, Cincinnati, OH 45242

TICA,   The International Cat Association, Inc., Office of the Secretary, P.O. Box 2684, Harlingen, TX 78551

In Great Britain there are two cat registering bodies :

The Cat Association of Great Britain, Mill House, Letcombe Regis, Oxfordshire OX12 9JD (Founded 1983)

The Governing Council of the Cat Fancy, 4-6 Penel Orlieu, Bridgewater, Somerset TA6 3PG (Founded 1910)

There are also two national associations each responsible for organizing cat shows of international importance. (There also are many regional and breed clubs that organize championship shows throughout the United Kingdom. For details contact the General Council of the Cat Fancy.)

The National Cat Club, Sec. Mrs. R. Gowdy, The Laurels, Rocky Lane, Wendover Dean, Bucks HP22 6PR

The Kensington Kitten & Neuter Cat Club, Sec. Mrs. H.J. Hewitt, The Braes, 160 Hermitage Road, Woking, Surrey GU21 1XH

Owners of Persians who are interested in joining specialist clubs can contact one of the general Longhair Clubs or Persian Specialist clubs catering for owners of particular colors of Persians such as the Red, Cream, and Tortie Cat Society. The details of both these types of clubs can be obtained from the Governing Council of the Cat Fancy.

The federation, FIFe (the Feline International Federation) has affiliated clubs in twenty-five countries in Europe, Asia, and Latin America, and in some of these countries there are FIFe Specialist Persian Clubs. Details of the affiliated clubs and specialist clubs can be obtained from the Secretary General of FIFe, Mrs. R. van Haeringen, Boerhaavelaan 23, NL-5644BB, Eindhoven, the Netherlands.

GLOSSARY

AACE: American Association of Cat Enthusiasts.

ACA: American Cat Association; the oldest American association.

ACFA: American Cat Fanciers' Association.

Alter: term used in the United States for castrated or spayed cats which are known as neuters in Great Britain.

Anestrus: period between the sexually receptive phases of estrus.

Angora: one of the original varieties of long-coated cats, originally found in Turkey.

Back crossing: term used when a cat is mated back to its parent.

Balanced: term describing a cat with good proportions in relation to the Standard for a particular breed.

Barring: striped pattern. A form of tabby marking, which is a fault when occurring in self-colored cats.

Best of Breed: a cat which in the judge's opinion, comes nearest to matching the breed Standard of all the cats in a particular breed. Normally divided into adult, kitten, and neuter categories.

Bi-color: having a patched coat pattern of white and another color; also includes white with patches of recognized tabby patterns and colors.

Bite: position of upper and lower teeth when the mouth is closed.

Bloodlines: the ancestors of a given cat; this expression is sometimes used inaccurately to refer to any cat produced by a particular breeder.

Break: a distinct indentation in the skull formation at the bridge of the nose, occurring just below, or at a moderate distance below a point in between the eyes. The break is usually more noticeable when viewed in profile.

Breed: a group of cats with similar physical, defined characteristics.

Brindling: when hairs of one color are interspersed with another color; generally considered a fault and undesirable in most Persian colors.

Brush: 1) The short, full tail of a longhaired cat; 2) to groom a cat with a bristle, nylon, or mixture of nylon and bristle brush.

CA: The Cat Association (Great Britain).

Calico: used in the United States to describe a cat which is basically a white with a mantle of black and red or cream patches covering the cat's back. This color is referred to as a tortoiseshell-and-white cat in Great Britain.

Calling: the cry made by a female cat when she is in season.

Carnivore: a meat-eating animal.

Castration: the neutering or altering of males.

Cat Fancy: a general term for cat registries, breeders, and exhibitors of pedigreed and other cats.

Cat flu: term commonly used to describe feline upper respiratory virus disease.

Cattery: a place where cats are kept either for breeding or for boarding, or for both purposes.

CCA: Canadian Cat Association.

CFF: Cat Fanciers' Federation (United States).

CFA: Cat Fanciers' Association, Inc; the world's largest pedigreed cat registry with members in Canada, Japan, Europe and South America. Incorporated in the United States.

Champion: a title earned by a cat generally by defeating other cats in competition while trying to earn a more important title (e.g. Grand Champion). In England a registered cat must defeat cats of the same breed in three Open Classes under three different judges to earn the title.

Classic: name given to the most usual of the tabby markings.

Club class: class at shows put on by clubs specifically for their members.

Coarse: a description used when a cat's fur tends to be harsh rather than silky or soft; or not smooth, refined, or harmonious in the overall picture of the cat.

Cobby: a cat having a short body, broad in the beam, and on short legs in proportion to the body.

Condition: the general state of health and fitness and well being which includes weight, muscle tone, cleanliness, radiant good health, and perfect grooming.

Conformation: the particular body form of a cat including the torso, legs, and tail.

Congenital: existing at birth but not acquired by heredity.

Cross-bred: the result of mating one pure-bred variety to another different pure-bred variety.

Cross: an imprecise term for mating two cats, generally implying that they are distinctly different in color and/or breed.

Dam: the mother cat or female parent.

Dilution: a lighter version of a standard feline color. For example blue is a dilute of black; cream is the dilute of red; and lilac (lavender) is the dilute of chocolate.

Doctoring: the common, essentially British term meaning "neutering." In the United States it is a term also used to describe the illegal alteration of a cat's color or conformation.

Ear furnishings: the hairs growing inside the ears.

Entire: not neutered.

Estrus: regularly recurring periods of sexual receptivity in female cats.

Extreme: pronounced; manifesting an exaggerated version of a desirable characteristic.

Fancier: a person especially interested in cats.

FCV: Feline calcivirus; a virus that causes upper respiratory disease (cat flu).

FIFe: Feline International Federation.

FLV: Feline Leukemia Virus.

Follicle: 1) the "pit" in the skin from which hair grows; 2) the sac on the female's ovary in which an egg develops.

Frill: ruff; the hairs around the head forming a frame to the face.

Furball: fur swallowed by a cat when washing, forming a sausage-like body in the stomach or bowels. It is usually regurgitated but in some cases it requires surgical attention. Also called hairball.

GCCF: the Governing Council of the Cat Fancy (United Kingdom).

Gene: the units in body cells responsible for passing hereditary characteristics from one generation to another. Each gene is responsible for one attribute. They control the growth, development, function, and physical characteristics of the cat.

Genetics: The modern science of heredity.

Genotype: the genes inherited by an individual from its parents which may not be visible in the physical appearance.

Gestation: Pregnancy; the period of time between conception and birth of the kittens.

Grand Champion: the title earned by a cat that is a Champion and that defeats a specific number of other Champions in competition. In The International Cat Association, this is the title earned by a cat that makes a specific number of finals and earns a specific number of points in competition.

Heat: a period of sexual receptivity in a female cat; estrus.

Hormone: a chemical messenger secreted into the bloodstream by a gland in order to affect development or function in another part of the body.

Hot: a term used when referring to coat color, particularly referring to cream when the color is too red.

Inbreeding: mating of closely related cats, such as parents to offspring, or brother to sister.

Kitten: a young cat; for exhibition purposes, a cat between the ages of four and nine months, or four to eight months in the United States.

Lactation: milk production.

Line breeding: a mating between related cats that share a common ancestor appearing at least once in the first three generations on both the sire and the dam's side of the pedigree.

Litter: kittens born at the same time from the same mother.

Litter registration: registering a litter of kittens with one of the cat associations.

Mackerel: a pattern of tabby markings, sometimes likened to the fish of the same name, with penciling or rings as narrow and numorous as possible.

Marbled: the usual pattern of tabby markings; also known as classic or blotched.

Mask: the darker coloring of the face on cats with contrasting points, as in colorpoints (Himalayans).

Monorchid: a cat with only one testicle apparent. Such cats may not be shown in most associations in the world unless altered.

Neuter: a castrated male, or a spayed female—usually known as an altered cat.

Nose leather: the skin covering of the cat's nose. The color varies, e.g. it should be brick-red in Chinchillas.

Odd-eyed: Eyes of different color in the same cat, usually one blue, and the other orange or copper.

Out-of-coat: lacking quantity and quality of coat. The coat during a moulting period.

Overshot: a malocclusion where the upper jaw overlaps, but does not meet the lower jaw.

Pads: the cushions on the soles of the paws.

Parti-color: having a coat of two or three distinct colors.

Parturition: the act of giving birth to kittens.

Patching: well-defined patches of coloring, as seen in the coats of tortoiseshell-and-white Persians (calicos).

Pedigrees: a chart showing the line of descent of a pure-bred animal.

Phenotype: a cat's physical characteristics.

Pigment: coloration in a cat.

Points: the darker coloring on the head, legs, ears, and tail.

Polydactyl: having six toes or more on the front feet, and five or more on the back feet (not allowed for show purposes).

Prefix: a unique word chosen and sometimes registered with a registering body, to precede the names of all cats bred by a given person.

Premier: a neuter equivalent of a Champion.

Pricked: describes cat's ears held up alert in the upright or forward posture.

Progeny: offspring.

Provisional: a class for breeds not yet accepted for Championship competition, but elegible for competition at cat shows.

Pure bred: a cat whose ancestors are all of the same variety. This is not a synonym for "pedigreed."

Queen: an unneutered female cat of breeding age.

Rangy: a cat either long in body and/or with long, slender legs.

Recognition: acceptance of a Standard for a new variety by the appropriate registering body.

Register: to record the details of a cat, kitten, or litter with a registering body.

Registry: an association that records the lineage of cats, issues registration numbers, licenses shows, etc.

Ring: an area in which cats are judged at some shows.

Rosettes: brightly colored arrangements of ribbon that consist of a round centerpiece to which several long strips of ribbon have been affixed.

Ruff: frill; the long hair around the neck, framing the face.

Sanction show: a show run in Great Britain on similar lines to a Championship show, but at which no Challenge Certificates are awarded.

Schedule: booklets issued by the club organizing a show, giving details of the various classes, the judges, the rules, and the regulations.

Self: the same color all over, e.g. the red-self, which is also known as the solid red.

Sire: the male parent.

Solid: *see* Self.

Spaying: the neutering or altering of a female cat.

Spraying: the male cat's habit of delineating its territory, leaving a most pungent smell around.

Standard: a written description of the specific characteristics for a recognized variety and by which the cats are judged.

Stop: an indentation in the bridge of the nose, occurring at a moderate distance below a point in between the eyes *(see* break).

Stud: male cat kept for breeding purposes.

Stud book: a volume containing the names, sexes, and colors of cats, their birth dates, and similar information (when known) about the cat's parents; records of wins at Championship shows.

Supreme: a title awarded to the winning adult, kitten, and neuter, at the Supreme Cat Show (United Kingdom).

TICA: The International Cat Association (United States).

Titles: ranks, based on merit, earned over time by a cat in competition.

Tipping: contrasting colors at the end of cat's hairs, as in the Chinchillas.

Tri-color: having three distinct colors in the coat, white being considered a color; also referred to as a parti-color..

Type: the characteristics distinguishing a breed. It is also used to describe the particular facial bone structure of a breed, i.e. the short nose and broad muzzle of a Persian.

UCF: United Cat Fanciers' (United States).

Undershot: when the lower jaw protrudes further than the upper jaw.

BIBLIOGRAPHY

Bush, Barry, B.V.Sc., F.R.C.V.S. *The Cat Care Question and Answer Book.* London, Orbis Publishing Ltd., 1981.

Carlson, Delbert G., D.V.M. and Griffin, James M., M.D. *Cat Owner's Home Veterinary Handbook.* New York, Howell Book House, 1983.

Champion, Dorothy Bevell. *Everybody's Cat Book.* New York, copyright © D.B. Champion, 1909.

Currah, Ann. *The Cat Compendium.* London: William Kimber & Co. Ltd., 1969.

Fireman, Judy, ed. *The Cat Catalog.* New York, Workman Publication, 1976.

Gebhardt, Richard H. *The Complete Cat Book.* New York, Howell Book House, 1993.

Hawcroft, Tim, (Hons.) M.A.C.V.Sc . *The Howell Book of Cat Care.* New York, Howell Book House, 1991.

Jones, C.H., Ed. *The Cat Journal,* vol. 111. Palmyra, New York, 1903.

Joshua, Joan A., F.R.C.V.S. *Clinical Aspects of Some Diseases of Cats.* Oxford, England, Alden Press, 1965.

Loxton, Howard. *The Noble Cat.* London, Merehurst Press, 1990.

Manolson, Frank. *The Language of Your Cat.* London, Marshall Cavendish Books Ltd., 1977.

Manton, S.M., F.R.S. *Colorpoint Longhair and Himalayan Cats.* London, George Allen & Unwin Ltd., 1971.

Mery, Fernand. *The Life, History, and Magic of the Cat.* New York, Grosset & Dunlap, 1968.

Mivart, St. George, Ph.D., F.R.S. *The Cat.* London, John Murray, 1881.

Pond, Grace, ed. *The Cat Lovers Bedside Book.* London, B.T. Batsford, 1974.

Raleigh, Ivor. *A Practical Guide to Cats.* London, Hamlyn Publishing Group Ltd., 1976.

Ramsdale, Jeanne A. *Persian Cats & Other Longhairs.* T.F.H. Publications, Inc., l976.

Sayer, Angela. Cats. *A Guide to Breeding and Showing.* London, B.T. Batsford, 1983.

Silkstone Richards, Dorothy. *Pedigree Cat Breeding.* London, B.T. Batsford, 1977.

Simpson, Frances. *The Book of the Cat.* London, Cassell and Company, Ltd., 1903.

Spies, Joseph R. *The Complete Cat.* New York, Prentice Hall, Inc., 1966.

The TV Vet. *Cats: Their Health and Care.* Ipswich, Suffolk, England, Farming Press Ltd., 1977.

Wright, Michael and Walters, Sally. *The Book of the Cat.* New York, Summit Books, 1980.

Each of the cat registries and associations listed on pages 211-212 publishes individual show rules, stud books, year books, and breed Standards. Readers can write to the secretary of each organization for a list of publications.

PHOTO CREDITS

Courtesy Gladys Barton: p.153. **Courtesy Cat Fanciers' Association, Inc.:** p. 146 bottom, 148 (photo by Ellison's), p. 161 center left (photo by Larry Johnson), p. 161 bottom right, p. 162 center left, p. 163 top (photo by Carl J. Widmer), p. 163 center left (photo by Chanan), p. 164 center left, p. 165 top, p. 165 center left (photo by Larry Johnson), p. 165 bottom, p. 166 top (photo by Jane Howard), p. 166 center left, p. 167 center right, p. 167 center left, p. 168 center right, p. 168 center left, p. 189, p. 192, p. 193, p. 194, p. 196, p. 208. **Courtesy the Governing Council of the Cat Fancy:** p. 117. **Sheila Harrison:** p. 168 top. **Marc Henrie:** p. 50, p. 51, p. 54, p. 59, p. 77 top and bottom, p. 78, p. 81, p. 82, p. 85, p. 86, p. 88, p. 106, p. 108, p. 111, p. 112, p. 115, p. 118, p. 123, p. 131 bottom, p. 161 upper right, p. 161 center right, p. 161 bottom left, p. 162 top, p. 162 center right, p. 162 bottom, p. 163 bottom, p. 164 top, p. 164 center right, p. 164 bottom, p. 165 center right, p. 166 center right, p. 167 top, p. 168 bottom. **The Illustrated London News Picture Library:** p. 10, p. 137. **Mirabel Books Ltd.:** p. 16, p. 74, p. 76, p. 89, p. 97, p. 157, p. 163 center right, p. 166 bottom, p. 167 bottom. **Courtesy Barbara Patch:** p. 198.

INDEX

A

abortion, 101
Abyssinian, 21
Acinonyx, 15-16
acquiring a Persian, 50-67
African Wild Cat, 16, 19
Alpaca cat, 22
American Cat Association (ACA), 47, 120, 148
American Cat Club, 23
American Cat Fanciers' Association (ACFA), 120, 126, 146, 152
American Curl, 21
American Wirehair, 21
amniotic sac, 105
ancestry of the Persian, 11-29
anestrus, 91
Angora, 11, 22-27
animal illustrators, 2, 10, 63, 138
animal rescue societies and shelters, 51-52, 87
Ankara Zoo, 23
Attenborough, Sir David, 17
Australian cat Fancy, 47, 59, 207-208
awards, 114-119, 131, 133-134, 141

B

Bailey, Anne, 200-201
Balinese, 21, 24
Bangs, Isobella, 191
Barrett, Michael and Brenda, 202
Bast, 12-13
bathing, 79-85
benching cages, 60, 114, 127-131, 134-135
bi-color Persian, 32, 45-46, 64, 116, 143, 149, 166-167, 169-171, 196-197
Birch, Leonie, 207-208
Birman, 21, 201
Birmingham cat show of 1907 (United Kingdom), 180
birth, 90, 100, 104-105
black Persian, 2, 31, 34-35, 37, 47, 60, 150-151, 161, 178, 192-193, 195, 209
black-smoke Persian, 41-42, 65, 155, 163, 176, 180, 195
blue-and-white Van bi-color Persian, 167
blue cat, 25
blue-cream-lynx-point (blue-tortie lynx) Himalayan (colorpoint), 173
blue-cream Persian, 149, 160, 166, 189

blue-cream point (blue-tortie-point) Himalayan (colorpoint), 172
blue-cream smoke Persian, 42, 156, 164
blue-lynx-point (blue-tabby-point) Himalayan (colorpoint), 172
blue-patched tabby Persian, 159, 165
blue Persian, 24, 27, 30, 35-36, 139, 150-151, 161, 171, 185-186, 189-191, 207-208
The Blue Persian Cat Society (United Kingdom), 35, 140-141
Blue Persian Championship Show (United Kingdom)
  of 1952, 189
  of 1955, 188-189
  of 1957, 188-189
  of 1958, 188-189
blue-point Himalayan (colorpoint), 168, 172
blue-smoke Persian, 156
blue tabby Persian, 43, 159
blue-tortie tabby Persian, 160
Borret, Anne and Ben, 199-200
Botanic Gardens cat show of 1908, 180
bran: used for grooming purposes, 84-85
breeders, 177-202. *See also* catteries
breeding, 87-90, 95, 121-122, 124
Brice-Webb, Dorrie, 185-186
Brighton Championship Show of the Cat Club of 1901 (United Kingdom), 127
British wild cat, 27
Brocato, Greg and Judy, 192-193
brown-patched tabby Persian, 159, 165
brown tabby Persian, 43-45, 159, 164, 181, 196
Brunton, Marguerite, 186-187, 193, 202
brush (tail hair), 148-149
Buchan, Irene, 195
Bull, Marjorie, 193
Burland, A., 37-38, 44

C

calcium, 101-102, 109
calico Persian, 45-46, 64, 143, 149, 169, 197, 207-208
California Silver Fanciers, 195
calling, 57, 91-92
cameo Persian, 153, 155, 195, 207
cameo-smoke (red-smoke) Persian, 42, 156

cameo tabby Persian, 160
Canadian Cat Association (CCA), 120
Capital Longhaired Cat Show (United Kingdom), 191
Carnivorae, 14-16
Carthusian Cat, 25
Cat Association (United Kingdom), 122
cat beds, 70-71, 74
cat carriers, 73-74, 96, 132
The Cat Club (United Kingdom), 141
Cat Fanciers' Association, Inc. (CFA), 19, 23, 47, 119-120, 125-126, 133, 143, 147, 151, 171, 205-206
Cat Fanciers' Federation (CFF), 120, 145, 147-149, 158-160
cat fossils, 14
catproofing, 53, 68-70
catteries, 58, 63, 178
  Allington, 181-183, 195
  Anneby, 200-201
  ANZ, 197
  Araho, 195-196
  Argent, 39, 179
  Bonavia, 183-184
  Briarry Cattery, 171
  Chermician, 196
  Chestermere, 199-200
  Cyrus Persian Cattery, 178
  Deebank, 193
  Dunesk, 186-187, 193, 202
  Finchfield, 202
  Foxavon, 190-191
  Gaydene, 188-189
  Gray Ivy, 195
  Hardendale, 195
  Honeycharm, 197-198
  Honeymist, 190
  Jemari, 184-185
  Kaiwan, 196
  Lafrabella, 191
  Mingchiu, 198-199
  Palmetto, 195
  Pathfinders, 197
  Pensford, 186, 195
  Rambo, 197
  Red Pine Cattery, 208
  Rodell Rex Cattery, 21
  Rojodanco, 201
  Romaldkirk, 37
  Ronada, 185-186
  Shawnee, 189

Silva-Wyte, 192-193
Silver Mesa, 193-195
Simbelair, 191
Smithway, 196-197
Snowhite, 189-190
Southpaw, 193
Wee Heather, 195
Walnut Hill, 194-195
cervix, 100, 104
Cesarean delivery, 104
Champion, D. B., 32, 48
Champion, F., 39
Chinchilla-golden Persian, 154-155
Chinchilla Persian, 39-40, 62, 83,
    142-144, 152-153, 180-181,
    183-184, 193, 195, 207
Chinchilla-silver Persian, 38-39,
    152, 154, 163, 179, 207
chocolate Persian, 150
chocolate-point Himalayan
    (colorpoint), 172
chocolate smoke Persian, 42
chocolate tabby Persian, 160, 206
chocolate-tabby-point Himalayan
    (colorpoint), 173
chocolate-tortie Persian, 42
chocolate-tortie tabby Persian, 160
chocolate-tortoiseshell Persian, 160
classic tabby. See tabby Persian
colorpoint. See Himalayan
colorpoint shorthair, 21
congenital malformations, 101
Conway, Betty, 196
Cornish Rex, 19
cream-and-white bi-color Persian,
    166, 197
cream-lynx-point (cream-tabby-
    point) Himalayan (colorpoint),
    173-174
cream Persian, 32, 37, 150-151,
    162, 178, 189-190
cream-point Himalayan
    (colorpoint), 168, 172
cream-smoke Persian, 42, 156
cream tabby Persian, 160
Creodants, 15
Crystal Palace cat show (United
    Kingdom)
    of 1871, 35, 137-139
    of 1890, 10
    of 1896, 181
    of 1908, 180
Cymric, 21
cystic ovaries, 57
D
Dalles Rex, 22
de Buffon, Comte, 24
Debutante, 47
Decies, Lady, 38, 63
de la Val, Lottin, 25

della Valle, Pietro, 24
Devon Rex, 19, 142
diarrhea, 101
diestrus, 91
diet, 100-102, 107, 109-111, 126
dilute-calico Persian, 143, 149, 169
disqualification, 144-145, 205
E
ear mites, 79, 93
eastern European cat Fancy,
    203-204
Edinburgh cat show of 1875, 138
eggs, 91, 99-100
Egypt, 12-13, 17, 19
ejaculation, 99
embryos, 101
endometritis (uterine infection), 92
estrogen, 91- 92
estrus period, 90-92, 96
estrus suppression, 92
European Wild Cat, 16, 19-21
exhibiting, 60, 113-122, 125-132
exhibition only entries, 60, 119-120,
    134-135
F
Fabri de Peiresc, Nicholas-Claude, 24
fallopian tubes, 100
famous Persians, 176-202
    Anneby Charisma, Gr. Ch., 200
    Anneby Enchantress, Gr. Ch.,
    201
    Anneby Iddy Biddy, Gr. Ch., 200
    Anneby Scallywag, Gr. Ch., 200
    ANZ Betty Boop of Pajean,
    Gr. Ch., 197
    ANZ Jeepers Creepers, Gr. Ch.,
    197
    ANZ Toy, Ch., 197
    Argent Glorious, 39
    Argent Splendor, Ch., 180
    Arisbury Aphra, Ch ., 183
    Birkdale Ruffie, Ch., 181
    Camber Suzanne, Ch., 189
    Chermicican Santa Fe, Gr. Ch.,
    196
    Chestermere Chahila, Gr. Ch.,
    199-200
    Chestermere Chen Soo, 200
    Chestermere Kinuba, Gr. Ch.,
    200
    Chinnie, 62
    Crystal, Ch., 33, 146
    Cyrus the Great, 178
    Dazzler of Dunesk, 187
    Don Pedro of Thorpe, 42
    Duffy of Allington, 181
    Fanci-Pantz Petti Girl of Araho,
    Gr. Ch., 195-196
    Finchfield Michael, Gr. Ch., 202
    Finchfield Showpiece, Ch., 202

    Flambeau of Allington, Ch., 183
    Foxavon Alaskan Superior,
    Gr. Ch., 190-191
    Foxavon Marina, Ch., 191
    Foxavon Sharon, Gr. Ch., 191
    Foxavon Teromaa, Ch., 191
    Foxburrow Tilli Willi, Ch., 183
    Francis of Allington, 195
    Fulmer Zaida, 38
    Gaydene Genevieve, Ch.,
    188-189
    Gaydene Rudolph, Ch., 189
    Giselle, 189-190
    Hardendale Carrioca, Grand
    Premier, 195
    Hardendale Enchantress, Ch., 195
    Hardendale Eugenie, Ch., 195
    Hardendale Nicholas, Ch., 195
    Honeycharm Jasmine, Supreme
    Gr. Ch., 197-198
    Jarien's Southern Belle of
    Rambo, Gr. Ch., 197
    Jemari Justine, Ch., 184
    Jewel of Dunesk, 193
    Johnnie Fawe II, 34
    Julio, 194
    Kewlocke, Ch., 176, 180
    King Kong, 185
    Lady Gay of Pensford, triple Ch.,
    186
    Lafrabella Oh Lala, Gr. Ch., 191
    Lavender Liberty Beau, Gr. Ch.,
    193
    Lee's Let the Sunshine In,
    Gr. Ch., 197
    Lord Kew Tangerine, Ch., 179
    Lord Sylvester, Ch., 40
    Mingchiu Chou-Lou, Ch.,
    198- 199
    Mingchiu Mandarin of Sahadi,
    Ch., 198
    Mingchiu Ptan, Ch., 199
    Mingchiu Sulafour, Ch., 199
    Octavian of Pensford, 186
    Orion of Pensford, Ch., 195
    Paintin' the Town Red II, 189
    Paris, 138
    Pathfinders May Flower, Ch.,
    197
    Peggy Primrose, 46
    Persimmon, Ch., 43
    Petie K., Ch., 178
    Pied Piper of Barbe Bleue,
    Gr. Ch., 193
    Puck III, 32
    Quicksilver's Cascade, Gr. Ch.,
    200
    Ragamuffin, Gr. Ch., 200
    Rambo's Rocky Mountain
    Sunrise, Gr. Ch., 197

Rob Roy II of Arrandale, 180
Rodney of Allington, Ch., 183
Rojodanco Diodante,
    International Premier, 201
Rojodanco Mrs. Whiskers,
    International Ch., 201
Rojodanco Prunell, International
    European Ch., 201
Rojodanco Star Trek, 201
Romaldkirk Admiral, 37
Romaldkirk Midshipmite, 37
Shawnee Antiseptic, 189
Shawnee Moonflight, Gr. Ch.,
    189
Silva-Wyte Trafari of J.B,
    Gr. Ch., 193
Silver Mesa Apache, 195
Simbelair Mapleleaf Sioux, 191
Sir Ronlore of Silver Mesa, Ch.,
    193
Snowcloud Crispin, Ch., 189
Snowhite Herald, Ch., 190
Snowhite Jewel, Ch., 190
Spero Stink Puff of Smithway,
    Gr. Ch., 197
Teufel, 41
Topsy of Merevale, Ch., 44
Torrington Sunnysides, 36
Tuam New Sensation, Gold
    Double Gr. Ch., 207
Vel-Vene Voo Doo of Silva-Wyte,
    Gr. Ch., 193
Vera of Allington, Ch., 182
Vigilant Mark, 193
White Aigrette, 177, 193
Windibank Patti-Kake of Azulita,
    Ch., 146
Wistaria of Dunesk, 202
fawn Persians, 37
flame-point (red-point) Himalayan
    (colorpoint), 167, 172
flame-(red) lynx-point (flame-point
    tabby) Himalayan (colorpoint),
    173
feeding, 53, 72-73, 101
Feline Immunodeficiency Virus
    (FIV), 93
Feline Infectious Enteritis, 132
Feline International Federation
    (FIFe), 21, 58-59, 64, 119, 121,
    143, 145, 147-148, 157, 160,
    172-174, 186, 203-206
Feline Leukemia Virus (FLV), 93
Felis, 15-17, 19
Felis catus, 16-17
Felis domesticus (the domestic cat),
    11-12, 17
Felis manul. See Manul
Felis silvestris libyca. See African
    Wild Cat

Felis silvestris silvestris. See
    European Wild Cat
Felis torquata, 16, 17
fertilization, 100
first American cat show, 23,
    137-138, 142
fleas, 75, 93, 125, 210
follicles, 90-91, 100
follicle-stimulating hormone (FSH)
    90
Fulvicin, 101
G
Gebhardt, Richard, 192-193
genetic mutation, 19, 21-22
gestation, 100
Goforth, Mrs., 171
golden Persian, 153, 155, 162
gonadotropin-releasing hormones
    (GnRH), 90, 100
Governing Council of the Cat Fancy
    (GCCF), 21, 32, 42, 47-48,
    60-61, 64-66, 116, 118-120, 122-
    125, 128, 141, 143-148, 151-153,
    155-158, 160, 169-171, 173-174,
    181, 207
Gowdy, Rosemary, 152, 184
Greisofulvin. *See* Fulvicin
grooming, 53-54, 70, 74-86, 89,
    128-129
grooming tools, 75-76, 80, 85,
    128-129
H
Harding, Mrs. *See* Manton,
    Mrs. S. M.
Hawaiian cat Fancy, 210
Higuchi, Bess, 209
Himalayan (colorpoint), 47, 64-65,
    116, 144, 149, 167-168, 171-175,
    198-201, 206-208
Hogan, Jean, 189-190
hormones, 90-92, 100, 105
Horner, Nikki, 189
Howes, Marlene, 190
Hoyle, Doreen, 195
Hugo, Victor, 11
Hunt, M., 33
Hyde, J. T., 23
hyoid bone and ability to purr,
    15
hypothermia, 104
I
immunization, 52, 132
India, 12, 24, 34
Italy, 24, 29
J
James, Robert Kent, 26
Japanese Bobtail, 21-22
Japanese cat Fancy, 208-209
Javanese, 21
Johnson, Dr. Samuel, 11

judging, 60, 113-125, 130,
    133-135, 139, 142, 144, 149,
    152, 184-185
K
kittening box, 103-105, 107
L
Langston, Evelyn, 181-183
Lee, Bill and Gayle, 197
Lichtenberg, Ptricia, 195-196
life span of the Persian, 52-53
lilac-cream Persian, 42, 169
lilac Persian, 42
lilac-point Himalayan (colorpoint),
    172
lilac smoke Persian, 42, 206
lilac tabby Persian, 160
lilac-tabby-point Himalayan
    (colorpoint), 173
lilac-tortie Persian. *See* lilac-cream
    Persian
lilac-tortie tabby Persian, 160
litter size of the Persian, 88, 107
litter tray, 53, 71-72, 103
London smokes, 35
London Zoo, 15
Lord Mayor's Chain, 26-27
lordosis, 91, 98
Lushington, Laura, 23
luteinizing hormone (LH), 91,
    100
Lynx, 15-16
M
mackarel tabby, 17, 21, 64, 158
Maine Coon Cat, 21, 32
Manton, Mrs. S. M., 171, 198-199
Manul, 16, 19
Manx, 21, 126
Marcel, 21
masked-silver Persian, 38, 40
mastitis, 109
mating, 57, 91, 92, 95-96, 98-100
McVady, Lily, 188-189
medroxyprogesterone acetate, 92
megestrol acetate, 92
metritis, 109
Miacids, 15
Mivart, Dr. St. John, 14, 22, 25
modern-type Persian, 47-49, 147,
    191, 204, 207, 210
Mohammed, 11
N
National Cat Club, (United
    Kingdom), 10, 32, 59, 63,
    141, 190
National Cat Show (United
    Kingdom), 58-59, 190
nesting box, 107
neutering, 56-57, 63, 92, 96-97,
    117, 119-120
Newsome, Audrey, 190-191

222

New Zealand cat Fancy, 116, 120-121, 206-207
nipples, 100-101, 103, 107
Norwegian Forest Cat, 21

O

odd-eyed white Persian, 34, 191
O'Hara, Joan, 195-196
Oliver, A. St. John, 23
orange Persian. *See* red Persian
Oriental Longhair, 21
ovarian cysts, 92
ovaries, 90-91, 99-100
Over, Grace, 195
ovulation, 99
oxytocin, 105

P

Pallas's Cat, 19-20, 27-28
Pallas, Peter Simon, 19, 22
panleukopenia vaccines, 101
Panthera, 15-17
parti-color Persian, 42, 46, 64, 143, 149, 160, 166, 169-170, 189, 197-198, 207-208
Pasht, 12
Patch, Barbara, 197-198
patched Persian, 64, 158-160
patched tabby Persian (torbie), 64, 158, 160
peke-faced red Persian, 151, 170, 197
peritonitis, 132
Persian angora, 23-24
Persian queen's reproductive cycle, 86-110
pet shops, 51-52, 102
pewter Persian, 153
pinking-up, 100
pituitary gland, 90-91, 100
placenta, 105, 107
Pocock, R. L., 15
poisonous plants, 53, 70
poisonous substances, 69, 103
pregnancy, 57, 99-102
premature birth, 104
preoestrus, 91
progestins, 92
progestogens, 92
purring, 15, 17

Q

quarantine
in Australia, 207-208
in Hawaii, 210
Queen Elizabeth Ruffle, 26

R

rabies, 210
Rag Doll, 21
Raleigh, Dr. Ivor, 123
Rambo, Jim, 197
red-and-white bi-color Persian, 167, 196

Red, Cream, and Tortie Cat Society (United Kingdom), 141
red Persian, 32, 36-37, 45, 150-151, 161-162, 179, 189
red tabby Persian, 159, 165, 196-197
registration papers, 63-64
reproduction, 87-111
Richardson, Douglas, 15
Richmond Show (United Kingdom), 139
of 1903, 113, 130, 141
ringworm, 101
Roman Empire, 13-14
Ronner, Madame Henriette, 2
Roper, Dr., 34
Royal London Institution for Lost and Starving Cats, 87
Russian Longhair, 25-27

S

Sacred Cat of Burma, 116
Saunders, Mr. and Mrs. George, 196
Scallan, Kathie, 207
Scottish Fold, 21
seal-point Himalayan (colorpoint), 167, 171-172
seal-tortie-lynx-point (seal-tortie-tabby point) Himalayan (colorpoint), 173
seal-tortie-point Himalayan (colorpoint), 172
self-colored Persian. *See* solid-color Persian
shaded-cameo (red-Chinchilla) Persian, 154, 163, 195
shaded-golden Persian, 144, 154-155
shaded Persians, 36, 38-41, 62, 65, 83, 142-144, 148-149, 152-155, 163, 179-181, 183-184, 193, 195, 207, 209
shaded-silver Persian, 38-40, 144, 154
shaded tortoiseshell Persian, 154-155
shampoo, 79, 82-84
shell-cameo (red-Chinchilla) Persian, 154-155
shell-tortoiseshell Persian, 155
Shirane, Madame, 208-209
Siamese, 21, 24, 40, 47, 90, 171
silver-patched tabby Persian, 158-159
silver Persians, 36, 38-41, 153, 209
silver-point Himalayan (colorpoint), 206-207
Silver Showcase cat show (United States), 195
Silver Society (United Kingdom), 39
silver-tabby Persian, 42-43, 47, 158-159, 164

Simpson, Frances, 43, 181
Smith, Helen and Leonard, 196-197
smoke Persian, 32, 40-42, 47, 65, 149, 155-157, 163-164, 176, 180, 195-196, 206
smoke-point Himalayan (colorpoint), 206-207
smoke tortoiseshell, 42, 156
solid-color Persian, 2, 24, 27, 30-32, 34-37, 42, 45, 47, 60, 139, 149-15? 155, 161-162, 171, 178-179, 185-193, 195, 207-209
Somali, 21
spaying, *See* neutering
sperm cells, 99-100
spotted tabby Persians, 64, 206
spraying (scent-marking), 56, 96
Standard, 26-28, 30-33, 41, 47-49, 62, 89, 114-115, 120, 124-126, 136-138, 142-175, 204-207
Steppe Cat. *See* Pallas's Cat
steroids, 101
Steyning cat show of 1908 (United Kingdom), 180
Stirling-Webb, Brian, 171, 199
stud cat, 93-96
stud fee, 95
stud quarters, 96-99
stud-service contracts, 95
Supreme Cat Show (United Kingdom), 59, 112

T

tabby-and-white Persian, 64, 143, 170
tabby Persian, 17, 21, 27, 42-45, 47, 64, 143, 147, 149, 151, 157-160, 164-165, 170, 181, 196-197, 206
talcum powder, 84-85
The International Cat Association (TICA), 120, 126, 145, 149
Thompson, Joan, 186
Thompson, Will, 48, 122, 195, 199-200, 206
Tiffany, 21
Tiyi, queen of Egypt, 19
tortie tabby Persian. *See* patched tabby Persian
tortoiseshell-and-white Persian, 46
tortoiseshell Persian, 32, 34, 44-45, 64, 149, 160, 166
traditional type Persian, 47-49, 147, 204
training, 52-53, 72-73
tri-color Persian. *See* parti-color Persian
Turkish Angora, 21, 23
Turkish Van, 21, 23-24
Turner, Denis, 207-208

Turney, Molly, 183-184
Twain, Mark, 11
U
ultrasound scan, 101
umbilical cord, 105, 107
Uncia, 17
Uren, Cheryl, 207-208
uterus, 104-105
V
Van bi-color Persian, 143, 149, 169-170
Van-calico Persian, 143, 170
Van-dilute-calico Persian, 143, 170
Van-tabby-and-white Persian, 170

veterinary care, 72-73, 79, 92-93, 96-97, 100-101, 104-105, 109-110, 125
Victoria, Princess (of Schleswig-Holstein), 32
Victoria, queen of England, 31, 138, 140
Vidal, H. F., 33-34, 36, 42-43
vitamin A, 101-102
von Linné, Professor Carl, 17
W
Wain, Louis, 10, 63, 181
Webb, Gwen, 193, 195
Weir, Harrison, 10, 25-28, 30-31, 46, 136-138, 141-142, 150

Westminster Show (United Kingdom), 141
of 1903, 46
Weston, Dory, 194-195
Weston, Lois, 191
white Persian, 32-34, 83, 146, 150-151, 161, 177, 189-191, 207-209
White Persian Cat Club Show (United Kingdom), 191
Wickham-Ruffle, Eric, 123, 141, 153, 204
Winslow, H., 25, 27
Woodifield, Norah, 197
World Cat Show (Australia), 59
Worth, Joyce and Bob, 201-202

224